Nobel Life

Conversations with 24 Nobel Laureates
on their life stories,
advice for future generations
and what remains to be discovered

Dr Stefano Sandrone is an Italian neuroscientist working at Imperial College London. He was selected as a young scientist at the 64th Lindau Nobel Laureate Meeting in Physiology and Medicine. He was awarded the Julia Higgins Award and the President's Award from Imperial College London, the Science Educator Award presented by the Society for Neuroscience, and the H. Richard Tyler Award, the Lawrence C. McHenry Award and the A.B. Baker Teacher Recognition Award from the American Academy of Neurology.

Nobel Life

Conversations
with 24 Nobel Laureates
on their life stories,
advice for future generations
and what remains to be discovered

Stefano Sandrone

CAMBRIDGE
UNIVERSITY PRESS

CAMBRIDGE
UNIVERSITY PRESS

University Printing House, Cambridge CB2 8BS, United Kingdom

One Liberty Plaza, 20th Floor, New York, NY 10006, USA

477 Williamstown Road, Port Melbourne, VIC 3207, Australia

314–321, 3rd Floor, Plot 3, Splendor Forum, Jasola District Centre,
New Delhi – 110025, India

103 Penang Road, #05-06/07, Visioncrest Commercial, Singapore 238467

Cambridge University Press is part of the University of Cambridge.

It furthers the University's mission by disseminating knowledge in the pursuit of
education, learning, and research at the highest international levels of excellence.

www.cambridge.org
Information on this title: www.cambridge.org/9781108838283
DOI: 10.1017/9781108974301

First published 2021

Printed in the United Kingdom by TJ Books Limited, Padstow Cornwall

A catalogue record for this publication is available from the British Library.

ISBN 978-1-108-83828-3 Hardback

To my fantastic Grandfather Renato,
whose Noble Life and golden advice
inspire me on a daily basis

Contents

Foreword

Leafing through the pages of this book and enjoying one anecdote or another, I get the feeling of looking over Stefano Sandrone's shoulder. He conducts conversations the way they take place at the Lindau Nobel Laureate Meetings: between people with strong personalities, with space for scientific discussions and the exchange of life experiences. Just like the Lindau Meetings, the twenty chapters of this book benefit from a successful combination of the different Nobel Prize disciplines. One encounters modesty, profound knowledge and broad horizons.

Nobel Life breathes the Lindau Spirit, and the work of our alumnus of the 64th Lindau Nobel Laureate Meeting fills us with joy. We are happy to support the project – like many other ideas that have been carried from here into the world over the past seventy years. By putting down on paper an example of the intensive exchange between the stars of science and the ambitious and successful young scientists, Stefano Sandrone also conveys an existential criterion for the future of science: the willingness to share time, knowledge and experience, to give advice and recommendations, and to make all this accessible to as many people as possible.

I hope that these ideas, written down especially for the future generations of scientists, will be widely disseminated across borders, cultures and generations – diversity in the best sense.

They can provide orientation: for one's own experiences as a researcher as well as for life in general; as mental preparation for the next scientific discussion (not only in Lindau); or even when fantasising about what to do if a telephone call were to wake one up in the middle of the night.

Countess Bettina Bernadotte
Lindau Nobel Laureate Meetings

Preface

It is a phone call from Stockholm that turns scientists into Nobel Laureates, and it is an invitation from Lindau that calls young scientists worldwide to join the Nobel Meetings on the shore of Lake Constance. I was twenty-six when I received my invitation. The first Lindau Nobel Laureate Meeting took place in 1951: two German physicians contacted Count Lennart Bernadotte af Wisborg, grandson of the King of Sweden. Together they invited Nobel Laureates to interact with promising scientists, give hope and strengthen the international scientific community after the Second World War.

Life stories, challenges, discoveries. The medal and the other side of the medal. This is *your* invitation: enjoy the journey!

Stefano Sandrone

1

The Periodic Table

Roald Hoffmann

As you set out for Ithaka
hope the voyage is a long one,
full of adventure, full of discovery.
Laistrygonians and Cyclops,
angry Poseidon – don't be afraid of them:
you'll never find things like that on your way
as long as you keep your thoughts raised high,
as long as a rare excitement
stirs your spirit and your body.
Laistrygonians and Cyclops,
wild Poseidon – you won't encounter them
unless you bring them along inside your soul,
unless your soul sets them up in front of you.

Ithaka by Constantine P. Cavafy

Professor Roald Hoffmann, during World War II, as a child, you lived in a ghetto and a labour camp. Then, you hid for fifteen months in the attic and the storeroom of a school-house. You were there with your mum and some of your family, and unfortunately only a few of those who weren't with you survived. What are your memories of those tough months?

I was five when I went into that attic and almost seven when I came out. My memory is not good, but I remember some things: geography games with my mother – her asking me how to get from Złoczów, the town where I was born, to San Francisco. And I had to name every sea we went through, every port where we stopped. I remember the sack of peas that served as my pillow. I remember my uncle Fromcie coming in sick from the forest, running a fever, with no way to call a doctor. My mother asked for a spirit lamp and some jam jars. She heated the air in them and put them on my uncle's back. We called it 'stavit banki'; in English it's called 'cupping'. I remember learning to read, in Polish. I remember looking out through the slats in a wooden window of the attic and watching the children come out at recess and play in the yard. They were always running out of my sight. That small window was our only window on the world.

In 1949 you moved to the United States, and in 1981 you won the Nobel Prize in Chemistry, along with Kenichi Fukui, for theories 'concerning the course of chemical reactions'.[1] In 2006, you dedicated a monument to the Holocaust in the town you came from, some twenty kilometres from that school-house. Nowadays, the storeroom is part of a chemistry class-room. How was it coming back to that place sixty years later?

It was deeply moving. My son came with me, and he had a five-year-old son. So both he and I could imagine what it was like for my mother to keep me quiet and happy for a year and a

---

[1] www.nobelprize.org

half. We owe her – and the family who hid us at great risk to their life – everything.

The Italian writer, chemist and Holocaust survivor Primo Levi in his book *The Periodic Table* wrote that:

> ...*the nobility of man, acquired in a hundred centuries of trial and error, lay in making himself the conqueror of matter ... I had enrolled in chemistry because I wanted to remain faithful to this nobility. That conquering matter is to understand it, and understanding matter is necessary to understanding the universe and ourselves: and that therefore Mendeleev's Periodic Table, which just during those weeks we were laboriously learning to unravel, was poetry, loftier and more solemn than all the poetry we had swallowed down in* liceo; *and come to think of it, it even rhymed!*

Looking back, as you're an author of popular science books and plays, what was your first love, Professor Hoffmann: science or art?
Primo Levi was a wonderful writer. My first love was science. To be honest, I don't think I was mature enough to understand art and poetry, and to feel their importance to the human spirit, when I was first exposed to the wonders of science.

Where is the boundary between science and art?
The boundary is never clear. Science and art share the essence of creation – yes, science is about creation, not just discovery. They both value craftsmanship and an economy of statement or intensity. They both reach out to others and share similar aesthetic principles. Both are driven by a desire to understand. But there are differences – art finds the universal in the particular. It is that drop of dew on that blade of grass in which a poet can see the universe. And art teaches us the uses of ambiguity, while science defines for itself the universe of unambiguous problems for which there is a solution. Which

is more important? You decide! Is there a solution for the end of love? Will there ever be one?

If you could choose one element from the periodic table and tell a story about it, which element would you choose and what story would you tell?
It would be silicon, for it is a wonderful example of something that's the same and not the same – that's just what Primo Levi wrote about in his 'Potassium' chapter of *The Periodic Table*:

> *I thought of another moral ... and I believe that every militant chemist can confirm it: that one must distrust the almost-the-same (sodium is almost the same as potassium, but with sodium nothing would have happened), the practically identical, the approximate, the or-even, all surrogates, and all patchwork. The differences can be small, but they can lead to radically different consequences, like a railroad's switch points; the chemist's trade consists in good part in being aware of these differences, knowing them close up, and foreseeing their effects. And not only the chemist's trade.*

Silicon is like carbon in its chemical properties. And it's also totally unlike it: carbon dioxide is an essential gas, silicon dioxide is quartz. *Pace* science fiction, there is essentially no biochemistry of silicon. But it's taken its revenge in the world of cultural rather than biological evolution: our IT is based on silicon, not carbon.

After studying and doing research at Columbia and Harvard, you moved to Cornell University, Ithaca, where you're still based. Over your career, quoting the title of your Nobel Lecture, you have been 'building bridges between inorganic and organic chemistry'[1] but have also enjoyed teaching. You taught first-year general chemistry almost every year until you retired. Is teaching the most rewarding and enjoyable part of your career?

Both research and teaching were rewarding; I would rather not single out one. But I will say that teaching introductory chemistry without a doubt made me a better researcher. I knew all about those beautiful partial differential equations of thermodynamics, but before having to explain thermodynamics without those equations, I hadn't understood thermodynamics. Teaching taught me how to explain things to a varied audience – of people who understood nothing, of people who understood everything, and all shades in between. That's exactly the state of the audience for my theoretical work. Theory is all about explaining, and there's a lot to be learned from teaching.

Besides your academic achievements, your ability to communicate science is outstanding. It ranges from the television series *The World of Chemistry* to the *Entertaining Science* events at New York City's Cornelia Street Cafe, to mention two examples. A 'simple' question: what is chemistry?
Chemistry is the art, craft, business and science of substances and their transformations. That's the macroscopic view. At the same time, it is the art, craft, business and science of molecules and their transformations – we see things microscopically and macroscopically.

Which is easier to define: the beauty of chemistry or the chemistry of beauty?
I'm not sure there is chemistry in beauty, unless you have in mind what goes into the make-up that makes an actress become more beautiful than she is. I think the beauty of chemistry is easier.

Is chemistry more similar to the Parthenon in Athens or Park Güell in Barcelona?
Oh, no question, Park Güell: complex patterns in the park, an entry that is not the same from any side, utility – people stroll in it, children play. That's life. The Parthenon was classic beauty, simple in its forms, although the chryselephantine Athena that stood in it was not so simple. The Parthenon's

present state evokes other emotions – sadness at that destruction, a sense of history.

What were you doing when you received the call from Stockholm announcing the Nobel Prize? What was your first reaction? Were you somehow expecting 'that' call?
In science, the Nobel Prize is never a surprise – and it is a surprise. But perhaps not for the reason you think. It is never a surprise because we have a well-honed system for recognition of good work in science through the literature. Within a year of our work's publication, the community let us know the work was important. It was of Nobel calibre. But then you realize that the actual selection process is a matter of chance, the reasoned opinions of a few Swedish colleagues. Let me put it another way: every year before the Nobel Prize date, friends and colleagues ask me who will 'win'. I give them a list of five fields, ten people. My track record over thirty years is that in one out of every ten years I've been right. I'm not stupid; I know my field. What this tells you is that there are ten times as many people deserving of a Nobel Prize in Chemistry as can be awarded the Prize. Ergo, the chance quality.

In the year I was selected, with Kenichi Fukui – my colleague Robert Burns Woodward, who surely would have shared the award, having died just two years before – the usual process of the news being leaked to a Swedish newspaper so that they could call you failed. Maybe they called the wrong Hoffmann. Anyway, I was in the garage, fixing a tyre on my bicycle. I had the radio on, and heard it on the nine a.m. news. I ran in to call my mother, because I knew that would immediately become impossible.

What is your advice for future generations of scientists?
My advice to young scientists is the following: don't allow yourself to be taken over by science – your interest in science is natural, and unless you put a check on it, it may quite naturally engulf you. Be sure to take as many courses in the humanities and arts, and in foreign languages, as you can. The humanities don't have clear-cut answers to the problems of

life, but at least they pose questions and leave you aware that the most important ones – of human existence – will not be answered by science. And that humility, empathy and human kindness play a role.

Oh, and even when it seems hard, take every opportunity to write and speak. Half of one per cent of us get by on brains alone. The remainder has to teach, explain, write and speak, and convince people that what we say makes sense.

How will chemistry as we know it today and the chemistry of the coming years be related to and deal with these three dichotomies: artificial versus natural, simplicity versus complexity and stasis versus dynamism?
Chemistry will continue to confound and mix up the natural/ unnatural divide. It will not become simpler – that's for dreamers who *want* the world simple (and politicians, yours and ours). And we will understand the microscopic detail in which reactions occur.

Can we predict how many and which elements will be part of the periodic table in fifty years?
We can. But those new elements will be boring and useless. Stefano, do you have children?

Not yet.
But you know what they can do with LEGO blocks. If you give them a new LEGO block tomorrow – one that lasts a millionth of a second after you hand it to them, and is radioactive, and never more than a million atoms of it made – do you think your children will build something new with that new block? What matters are not the building blocks, or atoms, but the dragons, castles and cars that kids build from them – the molecules.

We are at the beginning of the book and of our journey. What remains to be discovered, in two sentences? Which questions will scientists have to answer in the next fifty years? Where will the next breakthroughs come from?

Oh, Stefano! Would you also like to know what stock to invest in, and who will win the World Cup?

Italy, I hope!
I'm for Italy too! Much remains to be discovered, from the mechanism of memory to how to make controlled polymers in two and three dimensions. Scientists in the next fifty years will have to deal not necessarily with the best way to make a fibre stronger than one we have now, but how to do so in an environmentally friendly way, without polluting the environment and ourselves.

We will deal with many of these scientific topics along our journey. Not only the 'what' but also the 'how' of science.
The next breakthroughs will come from young people all over the world, from every nation and region, who look intensely for the detail of what they do, and, at the same time – yes, it's possible – for every possible connection to everything else. They will come from young people – and I love awakening the gleam of understanding in their eyes – who understand that ethics is as much a human invention as physics.

What do you mean? That you are confident that future generations will champion not only the chemistry of the periodic table but also chemistry among people?
I am hoping that the chemists of the future will look beyond their chemistry. You see, I have absolutely no doubt that their chemistry will be better than ours, their control of chemical reactions more precise, their ability to judge the microscopic structure of a molecule in a jiffy much improved. But ... what they will have to work hard at, and what I worry that their education is not helping, is developing an appreciation for the moral, social and artistic aspects of our life. Chemistry is easy; being human is not.

2

Eureka and Disney World

Peter Agre

Life is an unfoldment,
and the further we travel the more truth we can comprehend.
To understand the things that are at our door
is the best preparation for understanding those that lie beyond.

Hypatia

Professor Peter Agre, you were born on 30th January 1949 in Northfield, Minnesota. How was the young Peter as a student?

As a schoolboy in the 1960s, I was obsessed with geopolitical events such as the war in Vietnam and relations with the Soviet Union and China. I was also interested in the culture of the North American Indians. My favourite outdoor activities were wilderness canoeing and cross-country skiing. My friends and I began an underground newspaper that provided much entertainment but brought some disciplinary actions. Unfortunately, my attitude was not focused on traditional academics, and I applied my talents only where I was interested. Following a summer camping trip to Russia and Eastern Europe, I withdrew from high school, as I had sufficient background to attend university, and I never completed some high-school courses, resulting in a D in chemistry. Once in college, I focused on chemistry and did very well.

You attended night school before joining the college. How was that period of your life? Were you also working while studying?

To qualify for the high-school certificate, one must have credits for standard courses in English language and in government. The actual academic standard is very modest, so I attended night school for a few weeks to fulfil this formality. I had part-time employment driving delivery trucks while I was a student. In retrospect, it was a dreary time in my life and bolstered my interest in achieving something much larger.

You then joined Augsburg College in Minneapolis, where your father was one of the teachers. How was it having your father around in college? Did he directly teach classes to you?

My father was an excellent Professor of Chemistry and was fairly prominent at Augsburg. I was in his general chemistry class in the first year, and while I did very well, I was certainly not the best student. Since my father's reputation always preceded me, I was at times embarrassed. It made me pretty eager to move on to my medical studies at another institution – Johns Hopkins.

Linus Pauling, who won two Nobel Prizes, one for Chemistry and one for Peace, was one of your father's friends. Do you remember your meetings with him? What is your memory of him?

Pauling and my father served together on the Education Committee at the American Chemical Society. A most fascinating individual, Pauling even stayed at our home for a few days when he lectured in Minnesota following his 1962 Nobel Peace Prize. Cheerful, outspoken and bearing a sense of humour, he asked my siblings and me questions about our school subjects. When he asked my five-year-old brother what he learned that day in kindergarten, he seemed thoroughly amused when Mark answered, 'Nothing.'

What fascinated you about Linus Pauling, both as a teenager and as an adult?

Pauling was very friendly and outgoing. Meeting such a highly recognized Nobel scientist was exciting for my siblings and me, but also produced a large response from people throughout Minneapolis. Later as a medical student, I came to appreciate Pauling's important contributions to chemistry and medicine, as well as his pivotal role in achieving the international Test Ban Treaty that ended the testing of nuclear weapons in the atmosphere.

In 1970, you travelled alone throughout Asia for several months. What do you remember of that trip? Where did you go and in what way was that trip meaningful to your life?

Alone for months with a backpack and limited funds, I developed a sense of self-sufficiency, as I had the rare chance to experience life in East Asia, South-east Asia, South Asia and the Middle East. I saw first-hand the challenges faced by the rural and urban poor in these countries. Needless to say, it was a maturing experience and reinforced my interest in a career in global health. At the same time, I also grew to appreciate how fascinating the world is and how irrelevant material wealth is.

When your children were born, the whole family was living on your salary, and you decided to supplement it by working as a ringside physician at boxing matches.
The boxing events were brutal, but the people were fascinating. This introduced me to a part of society I'd never experienced, including famous former champions, but I also met many young fighters from very poor backgrounds who risked permanent injury fighting for relatively small prizes – usually only about $200. I became very good friends with an elderly African American gentleman, Mack Lewis, who personally financed and ran a gym for young fighters. Most of his athletes had no family support, and he became the father figure for many. Mack taught the young lads discipline – to arise at six a.m. each morning to go running. Before they were allowed in his gym for afternoon boxing ring workouts, he personally checked that the boys had finished their school assignments. One of Mack's boxers became a world champion, but I think he was proudest of his boxers who went on to college and achieved great success outside the boxing ring.

What was the most difficult moment in your life? How did you get through it?
Without question, the death of our third child, an infant daughter, was the most difficult time ever. Surviving as a family was made possible by the wisdom and loving fortitude of my wife, Mary. In the end, we became a very close family.

In that period, did you think about leaving the field of scientific research?
I must confess that I questioned everything at that time. But it may have been that my research provided the solitude and

purpose that I needed. I'm so glad that I had the opportunity to spend those years building a small laboratory programme and even making a few discoveries.

I know that you have a family tradition of visiting a different national park every year. In 1991, the park chosen by your children was Disney World. Then, in 2003, you won the Nobel Prize in Chemistry 'for discoveries concerning channels in cell membranes' or, more precisely, the 'discovery of water channels' called aquaporins.[2] How are these two facts related? Can we please have a brief account of your discovery?

In the late 1980s, we were studying erythrocyte blood group antigens that cause haemolytic disease of the unborn infant in RhD-negative women during pregnancy. During our purification of the Rh protein, we serendipitously isolated a slightly smaller polypeptide of unknown function. I asked numerous scientists for their ideas, but no one could help, and we were very frustrated. Finding the function of the smaller protein came at a most unlikely time. As my wife and I raised four children, our annual vacation was always a camping trip to a national park. The children loved these trips. One year, when we asked them which national park they wanted to visit on our next summer vacation, they all screamed 'Disney World'. So we visited the Florida Everglades and then Disney World, which is also in Florida. As the long drive back to Baltimore took two days, we stopped in Chapel Hill, North Carolina, where I visited my former mentor, John Parker, at the University of North Carolina. During our conversation, I described the new protein of unknown function that was abundant in erythrocytes and renal tubules, and had homologues in plants. I will never forget how John leaned back and smiled while he suggested that the new protein might be the

2 www.nobelprize.org

membrane water channel that physiologists had been searching for, for over a century. When we returned to Baltimore, we teamed up with John's former student, Bill Guggino, tested water transport, and discovered that the protein had extremely high water permeability. I am very grateful for serendipity and family vacations!

How and where did you come up with the name aquaporins?
At lunch with a few beers before our first public lecture about the newly discovered water channel at the 1992 Annual Meeting of the American Society for Clinical Investigation, my lab team and several friends were discussing the need for a functionally relevant name for the protein. Typically, proteins have names with Latin or Greek roots, so we put together combinations. The name 'aquaporin' just sounded right, and my Italian postdoctoral fellow assured me that this was indeed the Italian name for a channel for water.

You have often decided to openly discuss your results while performing experiments and to share them with colleagues. Were you ever afraid that someone else could have 'stolen' your ideas and beaten you in the race to publish?
As scientists, we have the opportunity to make novel discoveries, but not uncommonly this may require insight beyond our own. Had we kept our curiosity about 28 kDa [the aquaporin protein] a secret, we may not have solved its function as a water channel. However, once this was discovered, several other groups jumped in, so we had to work quickly and efficiently.

What were you doing when you received the call from Stockholm?
As the time in Stockholm is six hours ahead of Baltimore, I was in bed at 5.30 a.m. when the call came. Delighted with the news, I ran to the shower while my wife, Mary, called my mother in Minnesota. My father, a chemistry professor, had

died eight years earlier, and my mother, a former farm girl, lived alone. Her reaction was so genuine and practical: 'Mary, tell Peter that's very nice but not to let it go to his head.'

Back to Baltimore: a delegation from Christian Dior visited your lab. And this made your mum very proud, right?
Several years ago, the executives from Christian Dior visited my laboratory and invited me to give a lecture in Paris. Their chemists had discovered some small molecules that slightly induced expression of AQP3 [aquaporin 3] in sun-exposed skin. From this, they developed a new line of a skincare product, which was very expensive – approximately €50 for a fifty-gram jar. They offered some modest financial support for my laboratory, which I declined, as I would forever have to credit them in all of my lectures. The lecture in Paris was well attended and a lot of fun. Afterwards, I was shown a colour advertisement on the back of a French beauty magazine with a photo of their product and the face of a beautiful blonde young woman with water dripping on her cheek. The text claimed: 'Des résultats spectaculaires' and 'Le prix Nobel de chimie en 2003.' When I showed the photo to my dear old mother, a former farm girl who never attended university, she smiled and said, 'Peter, I think you are finally doing something useful!'

After winning the Nobel Prize, you came back to one of your first medical passions, haematology. What are you doing in southern Africa and how many months per year do you spend there?
My interest in global health brought new opportunities. Rather than restricting our lab to biochemical studies of aquaporins, I accepted the Directorship of the Johns Hopkins Malaria Research Institute. Part of the responsibility is to live and work with our field teams in rural Zambia and Zimbabwe for two to three months each year. I consider this to be the best part of my job.

What still needs to be done, and what strategies and approaches are needed, to definitively eradicate malaria in Africa? When will we be able to achieve this?

Malaria has always been a problem for the poorest countries. World Health Organization statistics show that the majority of malaria deaths worldwide occur in children in sub-Saharan Africa. Investments by the donor nations and governments of some African countries, such as Zambia, have improved the situation considerably by increasing the ability to rapidly diagnose and treat malaria, as well as efforts to prevent malaria transmission. Unfortunately, extreme poverty, political instability and corruption have reduced the efficacy of public health efforts in some countries with immense malaria burdens. Controlling and eliminating malaria from countries with huge indigent populations, such as Nigeria and the Democratic Republic of the Congo, will require massive efforts over long periods of time. We need better tools, such as an effective vaccine, and new and effective medicines. We also need to use existing interventions more efficiently.

Is there a link between aquaporins and malaria?

All life forms, including malaria parasites, have aquaporins. In our lab, we showed that the parasite's own aquaglyceroporin is necessary for full virulence in the red-cell stage of the infection.

What are your aims for the coming years?

Unfortunately, I have developed some health problems with Parkinson's disease and spinal arthritis that have restricted my activities. But my basic aim is to advance the fight against malaria in Africa and to use the opportunity that science brings to open doors worldwide through trips to places like Cuba, Iran and North Korea. When possible, we have invited the young scientists from these countries to Lindau to participate in the global community of science.

What is your advice for future generations of scientists?
While older scientists like me have a responsibility to support and encourage young scientists in their work, it's the young scientists who have the energy and creative spark to make discoveries. Certainly, a scientific career provides the greatest adventures, and the discoveries benefit everyone.

In 2008, you were about to run for the Senate in Minnesota. Why did you decide not to do so?
My interest in the 2008 Senate election was based on two things. The incumbent had become increasingly conservative and was disliked by the people of Minnesota. The Senate lacked a progressive member with scientific and clinical credentials. The expectation that huge finances were needed made it impossible to succeed. At the same time, I was offered the Directorship of the Johns Hopkins Malaria Research Institute, a wonderful opportunity with strong resources for success.

Why have very few science Laureates established positions in parliaments and senates around the world? Would that be a better way to have a more immediate impact on policy-making?
I am unaware of any science Nobel Laureates serving in parliaments and senates. But some non-Laureates have done very well for their countries. Angela Merkel has a doctorate in physical chemistry, and this is represented by her understanding of scientific issues such as global climate change. I'm optimistic that some of the students attending the Lindau meetings may become leaders of their home countries.

If you were President of the United States, what would be the priorities of your scientific agenda and how would you implement them?
I would make science a centrepiece of our government and appoint highly successful scientists to leadership positions. President Obama did this by appointing Steven Chu [1997

Nobel Prize in Physics] to be Secretary of Energy and John Holdren [former President of the American Association for the Advancement of Science] as his Presidential Science Adviser.

Did Linus Pauling consciously or unconsciously inspire you towards your scientific and diplomatic efforts?
Pauling inspired me in these ways and others. He was a genius who made countless important discoveries, including sickle cell haemoglobin. Pauling was also a relentless voice for science who spoke truth to the US government – even when they didn't want to hear it.

3

Flying High

Richard R. Ernst

You've never lived till you've flown.

Bessie Coleman

Professor Richard Ernst, you were born and raised in the Swiss city of Winterthur. At that time, the philanthropist Werner Reinhart and conductor Hermann Scherchen took the local symphony orchestra, nowadays known as the Orchester Musikkollegium Winterthur, to a top level. You enjoyed live performances by some of the greatest performers of all time such as Clara Haskil, Igor Stravinsky and Pablo Casals, to name just a few. What role has music played in your life? Was it ever your dream to become a composer or conductor?

Yes, indeed, this was a dream of mine. I wanted to be respected by the environment I was used to. I didn't know much about science then and had no goals of a scientific nature. I thought that music could be a suitable vehicle to ride towards recognition.

When and where did your fascination with chemistry start?

My fascination with chemistry started when I discovered in 1944 in the attic of our nineteenth-century home a box full of chemicals that belonged to an uncle of mine who died in 1923. I started to do experiments in a playful manner and hoped for unexpected results. Fortunately, our house and I survived, although I frightened my mother.

Do you remember some of the experiments you performed as a child?

I used strong acids to dissolve 'stubborn' minerals and materials that otherwise wouldn't dissolve. I mixed solid sodium hydroxide and water until it started to boil by itself. I produced black smoke by heating up organic compounds that were heat sensitive until I had to leave the room. I built myself a hood in the basement of the house, but it was much too small to catch all the exhaust from my experiments. Several times, I had to flee from the upper storeys to survive. I learned that chemistry is stronger than me, and I learned to respect the forces of nature.

Are there similarities between music and chemistry?

Surprises and unexpected excitements are essential in both fields. I was able to create a new world that didn't exist without me and before me. I felt like a 'creator'. Composing music was as creative as finding a new chemical reaction with unexpected results. In both domains, I found new excitements in worlds that belonged to me alone.

In 1962, at the end of your doctoral studies, you were feeling 'like an artist balancing on a high rope without any interested spectators'.[3] The new nuclear magnetic resonance (NMR) instruments that you built with your supervisor, Hans Primas, didn't work very well, and the company that copied the instruments went out of business. In 1991, you won the Nobel Prize.

I always felt a loner, not knowing whether my ambitious goals could ever be reached and whether they made sense in a broader view. My profession was full of risks, and I could have failed at any moment.

What were the key turning points during these twenty-eight years?

Each successful experiment gave me more self-confidence, telling me that my searching made sense and could add to the common knowledge of science.

At one point in your life, you and Kurt Wüthrich, a future Nobel Laureate, were living in two flats at the top of your scientific institute. Was this done to work more and have more interactions between the two of you, or were there other reasons behind this choice?

The major reason was the lack of space in our institute, rather than to increase interaction or collaboration.

During your banquet speech in Stockholm, you said that the presence of all the former Nobel Laureates attending the

---

[3] www.nobelprize.org

ceremony gave you the feeling 'of being carried by a swarm of wild geese, some real high fliers',[3] as in Nils Holgersson's tales, and that you were afraid of falling. Is the fear of falling still present at the highest point of a scientist's career?

I still feel like I've lost ground with my science and with my ambitions.

Talking about flying, where were you and what were you doing when you received the call from Stockholm? What happened after you got the news?

Indeed, this moment was well arranged by destiny. I was sleeping in business class of a Pan Am plane flying non-stop from Moscow to New York. I was going to receive the Horwitz Prize at Columbia University, together with my colleague Kurt Wüthrich, who was already waiting for me in New York. The captain came and woke me up to tell me the news. I was tired and wanted to continue to sleep. I was nearly jumping on the ceiling, as I didn't expect such a surprise. I then had to go to the cockpit of the plane and talk via radio to the Nobel Committee in Stockholm.

What were you thinking in the moments before receiving the Nobel diploma from the King of Sweden?

'Why is it just me who is asked these questions? I have many equally deserving colleagues. They have contributed at least as much as me.' There is a large group of scientists who should have been honoured in the same way.

Where do you keep your Nobel diploma and the Nobel medal?

I had them in a shoebox in my closet until I was asked this question on Swiss TV, and I went home rapidly to check whether the treasures were still there. In the meantime, I became more cautious, and I no longer answer this or similar questions.

Do you look at the diploma and the medal sometimes?
Never, except when somebody asks about them. But I no
longer tell them where I store them.

**What will be the future applications and developments of
NMR?**
There is virtually no disease where NMR can't increase our
understanding of healing. Brain disorders are the most difficult
to understand. Here, magnetic resonance imaging, or MRI,
provides more insight than any other tool. It allows us to
comprehend the detailed functioning of the complex functions
of the various parts of the brain. Indeed, all investigations can
be performed in vivo and give immediate answers that a
medical practitioner can interpret. MRI can be focused on
individual structures in the brain; it can even explore the
functions of individual cells or molecules. It gives us a direct
answer to whatever question we pose about our most complicated organ. Medical research can no longer be imagined
without this universal tool.

**You won the Nobel Prize in Chemistry in the same year that
Aung San Suu Kyi won the Nobel Peace Prize and Nadine
Gordimer the Nobel Prize in Literature. What should define
scientists' civic responsibilities? How should scientists act for
the benefit of humankind beyond the boundaries of the
laboratory?**
I liked to cross-link science and humanities. I was interested in
both fields, and I think it's important to build bridges between
disciplines. After all, they all emerge from human drives that
are relevant to society. A science prize opens doors and gives
the courage to express thoughts that one normally keeps to
oneself. One gains in self-confidence and becomes more com-
municative. One should open one's heart and listen to the
concerns of others who have had a more difficult life so far.

'Science + dharma = social responsibility' is the title of a documentary featuring your life. How would you define the three blocks constituting this formula: science, dharma and social responsibility?

Science means to understand the physical, chemical and biological foundations of natural appearances. Dharma comprehends all spiritual aspects of our existence. Responsibility defines the framework to provide sense to our endeavours and to what we're doing.

A Nobel playlist: what are three operas or songs that inspired you as a scientist?

Music ties in much more with dharma and our feelings than directly with science.

I know that your love for arts and science, and the combination of the two, is still massively present in your daily routine. A trip to Nepal in 1968 made you very keen on Tibetan painting art and further shaped your artistic interest for the rest of your life. What are you particularly interested in?

I like to explore some extreme forms of human activity. They are relevant for me and for society, as I just said. In this sense, art and science belong together and can't be addressed separately.

Which aspects of Tibetan culture fascinate you the most?

I'm particularly interested in the comprehensive view of Tibetan scholars who have a profound view of reality with all its secrets.

I attended one of your lectures about Tibetan art, and you showed part of your remarkable private collection of paintings (thangkas) and bronzes. What discoveries can you make by applying your Raman spectrometer to these artworks?

I used Raman spectroscopy to identify the pigments that have been applied by the painter. Often, one can make a rough dating by the fact that certain pigments were used only within a narrow time window.

I know you have a Raman spectrometer at home. Where do you keep it?
My Raman spectrometer is standing in my basement. It requires about three square metres of floor space.

Do you also study the components of chemical pigments, such as azurite blue (mthing) present in your artworks?
It's mainly the pigment identification that can be made via Raman spectroscopy. No further insight can be obtained.

Is your fascination for Tibetan art somehow linked to spirituality or, more generally, with the quest for further spiritual aspects of our existence?
Tibet is a mysterious country with many secrets that are not accessible by objective science. I like 'seeing beyond science'.

You have met the Dalai Lama. In light of your fascination for Tibetan art and its spirituality, what did that meeting mean for you?
For me, the Dalai Lama belongs to the most respected personalities I have met in my life. I have full trust in him, in his honesty and his wisdom. I never had the impression that he acts for personal advantage. I fully trust him. In addition, he has a very natural humour – he's always smiling. He has left the problems of our existence behind him. This is how I imagine a supreme being to be. I've never met anybody like him before. He is, for me, an example I'd like to follow, if I have the strength and the endurance for it.

What is your advice for future generations of scientists?
Follow your interests and motivations, irrespective of the expected reactions of your friends and colleagues. Research is an extremely personal affair, and you have to please yourself first of all. Have clearly defined goals but leave the avenues to

reach them wide open at first. Maybe you will make a discovery on the way towards the goal. Your gifts are presents from nature, and you're responsible for taking advantage of them and exploiting them to the advantage of humanity. Gifts can be burdens, but they allow you to reach goals that others might not be able to achieve. Behave in a responsible manner!

4

I'll Show You What a Woman Can Do

Françoise Barré-Sinoussi

My mustrious lordship, I'll show you what a woman can do.

Artemisia Gentileschi

The first cases of AIDS date back to 1981. Only two years later, together with your mentor Luc Montagnier, you isolated the human immunodeficiency virus (HIV) causing AIDS. For this achievement, the two of you won the Nobel Prize in Medicine in 2008. Almost thirty-three million people have died from AIDS-related conditions worldwide, and more than seventy-five million people have become infected with HIV.[4] Professor Françoise Barré-Sinoussi, when you discuss HIV/AIDS with people who don't suffer from this disease, what are the things they don't know or are misinformed about?

A good proportion of people think that HIV isn't a problem anymore, there is a treatment for this chronic condition and there is nothing much to worry about. As a consequence, a significant proportion of young homosexual men are taking risks again. In France, my country, we've seen an increase in the incidence of the infection in the last years in the young homosexual population. I know there is a similar situation in the United States, Australia and other countries. The first point probably is that communication is not as intensive as it was in the past and is not as good as it should be. Some people think there is a cure: however, we know that the treatment is a life-long treatment; it's not a cure. There's a lot of work to be done regarding information about HIV.

There is also a significant proportion of people who are affected by HIV, but they don't know it because they have never asked to be tested. Thousands of them are infecting others, which is, of course, not optimal for ending the HIV epidemic. This is the situation in many countries around the world.

The general public also thinks that this is now mostly a disease of sub-Saharan Africa. They're not interested because they think they can't be affected, which is wrong because the

---

[4] www.who.int; www.unaids.org

virus travels all over the world. If the effort regarding access to prevention, care and treatment for everyone in the world doesn't continue, I would be worried about the future re-emergence of an HIV epidemic.

You've been to African and Asian countries many times. Your first visit to an African country was in 1985, when you went to Bangui for a World Health Organization work-shop, and the Nobel call surprised you when you were in Cambodia. What were your emotions during these visits? What are the moments that stick in your eyes and your heart after over thirty years of travel there?
That's a difficult question. The first time I went to Bangui in the Central African Republic in 1985, the participants of the meet-ing visited the hospital in the capital. We saw that many people in the hospital were in terrible, awful conditions. In 1985, there was no treatment for HIV, and not even medications for helping patients to die. It was a shock for me and for many of us at that meeting. We realized we had a responsibility and a duty to try to improve the clinical situation in those countries via lots of interventions, including training and transfer of knowledge. That's how I became involved in resource-limited settings.

I was trained at the Pasteur Institute in Paris. At that time, I fully understood what Louis Pasteur had in mind when he decided to implement the Pasteur Institute in different coun-tries in the world. Part of the activities was about transferring our knowledge and working *with* them, not just *for* them. This involved implementing research and intervention to improve the lives and dignity of people in resource-limited settings. There are plenty of things to be done. However, we can see some progress in resource-limited settings and in terms of the research done directly on site by African colleagues or col-leagues from South-east Asia. The results of implementing these structures and strengths benefit the population locally in terms of HIV and other diseases.

Many medicines are still not widely available in every country worldwide. What actions need to be taken to make access to healthcare universally available and to improve global health systems?

The so-called first-line treatment for HIV is and can be available everywhere. In principle, all patients can have access to first-line treatment in developing countries. If they don't, it's because they have not been tested for it. In most resource-limited settings today, when the patients are diagnosed, they're already at a very late stage of the disease. They arrive at the hospital and have infections: we know this is not the best situation for the treatment to be efficient. For me, the first priority is to test people in resource-limited settings.

It's easy to say, but not so easy to do. There are many obstacles: often people say it's a question of money and funding, but it's not just this. It's a question of testing for HIV: in small villages, they haven't got the professionals to do this. This means that we have to organize community-based activities for the communities themselves to be trained and to do the testing. We have tools that are very easy to use, for example rapid tests or first testing that can be used in small villages. If we have communities involved, we can improve the situation. We also need to have political weight: there are countries without access to medication because the politicians think that people affected by HIV don't deserve any treatment or medical care. They belong to what we call the 'key affected population': they are homosexual or drug users. Such politicians think they don't have to spend any money on this.

We have more than seventy countries in the world that have repressive measures against these populations: against homosexual people, drug users, sex workers, transgender people. And we know that repressive measures oppose accessing prevention, care and treatment. The list of obstacles is quite long.

There are also political issues, stigma and discrimination. When people are stigmatized, they don't want to have a test because they're afraid of being rejected by others, of being put in jail, of being rejected by their friends and family. Everyone can be affected by a disease like HIV. We have seen that for Ebola: populations were escaping and going into the forest because they were afraid of being considered to potentially carry Ebola. It is a process of education, organization of the health system and political will.

Stigma and discrimination are often associated with diseases, and they're constantly associated with HIV/AIDS and mental health. In 1996, for around a year, you didn't attend HIV/AIDS-related conferences.
In 1996 I wasn't going to conferences anymore because of the evolution of these conferences. I was at the first one in 1985 in Atlanta and at the second one in Paris in 1986, which I organized. Then, I went to the conferences in Washington, Stockholm and Montreal. At some point, these conferences became much more oriented towards political issues, the media and communities, but very little towards science. For these reasons, I stopped going for a while. Then, in 2000, the conference was organized in Durban, and there was a call from the international community saying: please come to Durban because in South Africa there's a terrible issue with the President, Thabo Mbeki, who doesn't recognize that HIV is the cause of AIDS. As a consequence, the magnitude of the epidemic in South Africa was enormous. And it was continuing to grow in some regions with more than fifty per cent of people affected by HIV without any access to care and treatment. When I decided, I said, 'OK, they're right, we should go there and put pressure on the government to change their policies.' I realized that those conferences could put pressure on governments to change their policies. Since 2000, I have been to these conferences every two years.

Mental health issues in academia still seem to be taboo.
A study at the University of California, Berkeley found that
forty-seven per cent of graduate students suffered from
depression, following a previous work that showed ten per
cent had contemplated suicide.[5] Have you ever experienced
depression in your life, and, if yes, how did you go through it?
I have experienced depression, but it wasn't related to my
research in academia as such, but rather to the field I was
working in, HIV. I went through a terrible period, and
I wasn't the only one. Even as a scientist, it was the first time
in my life that I'd been in contact with the patients. I saw
patients in terrible, awful conditions, dying from the disease on
which I was working. Some of them became my friends and,
unfortunately, died. As a human being, it was a very painful
experience. As a scientist, it was very stressful because I felt
responsible for trying to find a solution as fast as possible. But
as we know, science takes its time. There was a discrepancy
between my feelings as a human being and my feelings as a
scientist. In 1996, data from the retroviral treatment showed,
for the first time, that patients treated with a combination of
drugs could live with HIV. After that I had depression myself –
probably because it was the end of this terrible pressure on
our shoulders.

Thanks for this. I'm sure this answer will be of help to many
people suffering from mental health diseases. Next question:
there have been almost thirty years of legal issues ...
[Françoise interrupts me.] Not thirty years . . .

About twenty-five?
[She laughs.]

---

[5] S. Jaschik (2015). The Other Mental Health Crisis.
www.insidehighered.com/news/2015/04/22/berkeley-study-finds-
high-levels-depression-among-graduate-students; The Graduate
Assembly (2014). Graduate Student Happiness & Well-Being Report
2014. http://ga.berkeley.edu/wp-content/uploads/2015/04/
wellbeingreport_2014.pdf

[Dear reader, a brief recap. In 1984, Robert Gallo and his laboratory, with whom Françoise was, at that time, exchanging research samples, isolated the virus causing AIDS. However, it was the same virus that Françoise and Luc Montagnier had isolated one year earlier. Over the years, Gallo has kept contributing to HIV/AIDS-related research, but was not awarded the Nobel Prize in Medicine in 2008 that Françoise shared with Luc Montagnier for the 'discovery of human immunodeficiency virus'.[6] The third recipient was Harald zur Hausen 'for his discovery of human papilloma viruses causing cervical cancer',[6] – something unrelated to HIV/AIDS. Let's come back to the question.]

Almost thirty years of battles and disputes have taken place, including a joint declaration from the US President Ronald Reagan and the Prime Minister of France Jacques Chirac, mostly about the priority of discovery and the patents related to the test to detect the virus. How have you managed not to be distracted by these issues and to stay focused on your life and your research?

I stayed out of this story as much as possible because I wasn't interested in it. I'm a scientist, and as a scientist – and as a human being – I could see what was going on with the patients. My priority was to continue working and doing my best to enable progress for people affected by this disease. It's a sad story, in my opinion. I went to a meeting on the history of HIV in the US, at Cold Spring Harbour, with Bob Gallo: we were together without any problem. Indeed, I was invited by Bob Gallo himself, so the story is over. I said to a journalist who was asking why I didn't mention the conflict between the US and France, 'Why should I mention it? Why? Tell me – has that story affected the progress of science?' No. I'm a scientist and I'm only in charge of science.

---

[6] www.nobel.prize.org

Do you think Bob Gallo should have been awarded the Nobel Prize as well?
It's not for me to say anything about that. It's a question and a decision for the Nobel Committee. I respect their decision, and I have no opinion at all.

I know you've spent many Saturdays in the lab.
Not only Saturdays, but also Sundays and nights. [She laughs.]

On your wedding day, a Saturday, your fiancé had to call you in the laboratory to make sure you were joining him for the celebration. Well, that is dedication!
My fiancé knew me very well, obviously, and he wasn't surprised at all. He used to say, 'I know very well that the first priority in your life is your work, secondly your parents and then your cats, and I'm in fourth position.' He was very conscious of this when he married me and not surprised at all to have to call me in the lab on our wedding day. He knew that my dedication was mostly to the work I was doing. I have some difficulty in calling it 'work' because it's been a real passion for me.

In August 2015, you had to retire from active research. Were you looking forward to this or, as I can imagine, would you have never retired? Were you prepared for that stage of your life?
I was very well prepared – at some point in your career you have to retire. But that doesn't mean that you have to stop all your activities. My agenda is terribly full and, except that I don't have a lab anymore, I still have exactly the same activities I had before. I'm not doing science by myself anymore, but I still have relationships with scientists, I'm still coordinating and sharing a tour of the HIV Cure Project in many cities worldwide. If I had to totally retire and stop having any relationship with the scientific and HIV community, that would be difficult, but it's not the case. My former

collaborators are continuing their works. We prepared for my retirement for more than five years. I know they're producing very good science. It makes me happy to see my former collaborators at a very good level internationally. That was part of my job: to train a new generation of scientists. By looking at their results, I think I did that successfully. You shouldn't always think about yourself: as a scientist, you should be a leader, but you should also have the leadership to facilitate training and development of a new generation of scientists. I believe I did my job.

I completely agree with you. Do you think there is a right moment to take a step back from active research?
It's something that is progressive throughout your scientific life. As a young scientist, you work on the bench to find an answer to scientific questions. Initially, most of these questions are those your mentor asked you to work on. After your PhD, you start asking yourself scientific questions. Then, you start to supervise students. When you become a senior researcher, you also have an administrative role and make grant applications for the lab and for the young scientists working with you. It's a progressive process. The more bureaucracy and administrative work you have, the less you're at the bench: you can't do it all. The senior people become coordinators of the research in their lab, ensuring that everyone is working in a common direction, even if different models and approaches are being used, and also developing a collaborative network. Communication about research is important for their lab to be recognized and to have more access to funding. The public shouldn't think that a scientist is always in the lab with a lab coat on. The career of a scientist evolves from a student to a senior researcher in charge of laboratories.

A flashback to the beginning of your career: before completing your PhD, you started seeking advice from senior scientists at the Pasteur Institute. One of them told you that, as a

woman in science, it would have been better for you to choose a different career, as, he said, women are only good at caring for the home and babies. What is your message for the men who still behave and think in this awful way?

My message is that they're totally wrong, and there are plenty of examples that have shown that this kind of statement is totally false. We're talking about almost forty years ago, when this kind of mentality was everywhere, not only at the Pasteur but in many research organizations in France and outside France. Fortunately, it has evolved. When I started at Pasteur, there were fewer than five women as professors. Now, about fifty per cent of professors are women. Such progress has been possible because women demonstrated to men what they were capable of doing and, fortunately, are recognized today.

It's not easy to be recognized. For young female researchers, being recognized will probably be twice as hard as it is for men. But they should be persistent.

Any other thoughts or advice for the female scientists still suffering from sexist issues?

My advice to female scientists is to become a scientist because of their passion, as it has been for me, for giving to others. Because giving to others, and giving to patients in the field of biomedical sciences, is so important for *your own* life. If you live for yourself and just do science to produce publications and to have a wonderful CV, it's not enough.

The most important thing is to try to give as much as possible to others. In the field of medical sciences, this means to improve the life of patients suffering from diseases, whoever they are and wherever they are. If they have this passion, they should just keep going, because they will receive so much in return from the people they'll meet all over the world. In my case, I'm quite happy in life because I've tried to give the best of myself. When I go anywhere in the world – Africa, Cambodia, Vietnam – I'm so accepted by the populations, and *they* make me happy. To see a person affected by HIV, for example, who is alive, smiling, playing, dancing – that's the best gift for someone who, like me, has worked for so many years on this disease.

5

Toys' Stories

Aaron Ciechanover and Edmond H. Fischer

You can discover more about a person in an hour of play
than in a year of conversation.

Plato

Professor Aaron Ciechanover, when we met in Stockholm in 2014, you told me that you have a great collection of toys. How big is your collection and what are the items to which you are most attached?

I collect toys, and mostly toys that have something to do with me: either ones I had as a child, or something that reminds me of the cars and trains I used to take or airplanes I flew with. The purpose is to remind me of childhood and of what I've done during my life in a simple way, instead of, for example, taking photos. Different people have different ways of remembering. In Italy, in the old city of Bergamo, where we first met at the BergamoScienza science festival, there's a beautiful toy store that sells wooden toys. I love wooden toys because they're simple. They're not detailed. They only give you the shape and leave the rest to your imagination. That's the purpose: remembering different events in life. This simplicity leaves a lot to our imagination.

Will you display your collection for the public one day?

I don't think so; it's very personal. Each piece talks to me, as there's a story behind it. Why would the public be interested?

By the age of sixteen, you'd lost both your parents. Where did you find the strength to carry on?

It is very difficult to go back and say that you were a hero and you did this and that. I just did it. I was deteriorating a little bit. Now I look at it as mischievous, but, at that time, I was on the edge of delinquency. I was stealing little things. Several people were instrumental in putting me back on track: one was my brother who adopted me, and the second was my sister-in-law who died some years ago. My brother is still alive and in wonderful shape; we meet frequently. He's fourteen years older, so I was lucky in that sense, and he already had a home. The other one was my aunt: she was a widow, alone, and she took me into her home, so I immediately had a place to stay. Between them, all of a sudden, I discovered that I wanted to become a doctor, to go to medical school, and that I was interested in biology. It is hard to remember what I thought internally fifty years ago, but you certainly need good people around you. And I was lucky to have them around me.

There was a strong will on your side: you managed to realize your dream of becoming a doctor and then doing research.

Yes, but this is only something you can appreciate in retrospect. At that time, you didn't think about science, a career and discoveries; you only think about that now. Only in retrospect can you say I had strengths. I don't look at myself as a hero or anything like that, or that I fought the devil.

After your medical studies, your PhD and your successful postdoctoral training at the Massachusetts Institute of Technology, you managed to get an independent academic position at the Faculty of Medicine of the Israel Institute of Technology, the same faculty where you graduated. Since then, you've spent most of your academic time in Israel. You were about to open your laboratory, establish your own group and start your research programme: a great deal of responsibility. What were your feelings at that time?

It's the same responsibility that young scientists in the world have when they come back. Not every country has mechanisms to absorb people back. I know that your country is a little bit different – I don't know if I would have been that successful in Italy. In Israel, even today, we have many problems with democracy, but Israel has a well-oiled mechanism of bringing scholars back to university. We want them to go away for a while, typically for the postdoctoral period, to be exposed to science in large institutions worldwide. We've evolved a good mechanism in terms of starting funds and tenure-track positions in the universities. Obviously, I had offers in the United States – even from a much better place compared with where

I am now. My institute is a good one, but it's not the best and not even among the best. But there were many reasons to come back, mostly historical, linguistic, cultural and family. Science is international and sometimes you don't care where you are: you go where you can do the best science. But we're human beings, and we're driven by other things as well, such as, for me, the history of my people here in Israel, my family, my language. It was difficult, but not impossible. Again, we're looking back at this: you don't plan success, you don't know where to go. You do it because you feel internally it's the right thing to do.

You came back to the same university where you'd been studying.
Yes, I even came back to the same department. But in the old days, it was still a relatively young country and this was customary. Even now, people complain about this kind of 'scientific inbreeding'. Today, we try to refrain from it, not only to avoid cultural inbreeding but also to avoid nepotism: the fact that the mentor brings the students back is not always 'academically healthy'. Although I came back to the same department, I developed my own independent research and moved to a different system and a different way of thinking. At that time, nobody in the world was working on ubiquitin; it was a neglected research area in 1984.

You won the Nobel Prize in 2004 for the discovery of ubiquitin-mediated protein degradation,[7] a sort of recycling system within the cells of our body. Before going abroad, your idea was to come back one day, sooner or later.
I thought so, but you never know. I was tempted to stay in the States: I looked at two academic positions there, and I got offers to stay. I hadn't really decided, but it's about the long-term future: where you want your children to grow up, or where you want yourself to play a key role. When you observe

---

[7] www.nobelprize.org

Israelis from abroad, you see that they keep close ties with their country; they read their newspapers and listen to Israeli radio. We're a minority, like the 'Little Italy' you see everywhere you go.

I know.
It was about our own food and other things. I didn't want to have just a 'Little Israel', but Israel itself.

I fully understand what you say: I live in London and, with my friends, we've set up our own 'Little Italy' too.
People should go wherever they feel is good for them. There are no rules or judgemental aspects of this. People should live wherever they feel comfortable.

Ten years after winning the Nobel Prize, during the Nobel Week in Stockholm, you told me that the aim of a scientist should not be winning the Nobel Prize but making great discoveries.
To live just for the Prize would be crazy. Think about the chance one has of getting a Nobel: one in one million or something very close to this. If the Prize is what drives someone, this is a negative drive. I think that the purpose of life is to enjoy life itself. But if you define enjoyment by doing something of high quality, you need to have an insight into what you do. You need to be very judgemental. Obviously, you have to decide what is good science by looking around, comparing and judging: you want to be original. It's a matter of internal judgement and insights into what you do. Being driven by prizes and recognitions is a negative drive. The prizes will come. Prizes are tools that society has developed to pay tribute to someone, but they have nothing to do with science. We rarely solve a whole scientific problem in our lifetime. We solve a little bit, and someone else will solve another bit. There are, of course, great discoveries that are founding stones. I don't know much about physics and if I had to explain what Einstein did, that would be difficult for me . . .

Indeed!

But everybody knows about relativity and knows that it changed the universe. Concerning biology, I know what the founding stones are. For example, the discovery of the double-helix structure of DNA, on which other discoveries have been built, from mutations to the ability to change and understand the flow of information. It is huge, in retrospect. But I don't think Watson and Crick immediately foresaw the consequences of what they had done, or how many further Nobel Prizes would be awarded for DNA-related discoveries. When people make great discoveries, they can't see them in their entirety: this takes time in science. Science is about laying one stone on another and then another. The only problem is that you must be sure that the stones are strong enough to hold up the rest of the building in the future, because if there is a weak stone, it will not support it.

I know you're actively and remarkably engaged in teaching science to children in schools. How wonderful are these classes with kids?

I love it. I see it as a mission, because there's nothing like seeing, and seeing is believing. You tell them a story and the first thing they see is that you're a human being: you walk, you talk, you're not an ET, somebody from outer space. You speak their language, not Oxfordian Hebrew. They see it *is* possible. It's about doing something meaningful for society, and it's not about the prize. Don't think of the prize, but of making something good and of high quality that will impact on people. They see that all of this is possible.

What are the most important things you've learned in your life so far?

That you shouldn't have a purpose. Instead, you should think of life as a collection of enjoyable experiences, and then you go from one experience to another. Because if you have a purpose, let's say 'to make a million dollars', once you get it, you'll want to make the second million, and then the third and the fourth. You should just enjoy life. And if you think of each experience in terms of what you learn from it, and how to improve it, then you enjoy life. For me, life is enjoyment: it's a journey of exciting adventures. Many people around me are bored, even though they're in good careers. They go to work every day and look at their watches; they go home or to the pub or wherever they go. With a life in science, there are no limits. It surrounds you all the time. I've been in science for more than forty years and it's just great!

What is your advice for future generations?
Not to get stuck with something. I was a physician and I started surgery. Then I stopped and became a student again at the age of thirty and started science almost from the beginning. Why? Because I felt that being in medicine, as a doctor or a surgeon, wouldn't have satisfied me for the next fifty years. We are living longer now, to the age of eighty or ninety.

I was a good friend of the Nobel Laureate Rita Levi-Montalcini, and she lived for 103 years. She was absolutely amazing: one of the most amazing people I've ever met in my life.

We're living longer, and it's stupid to study medicine or to do something for the next fifty or sixty years just because someone told us to do it. Young people should close their eyes and think about what they like and what they want to do for the rest of their life. It's not about making money; it's about enjoying the future. Don't get stuck: there are so many years ahead of you. Do what you love, whatever it is: being a dancer, an architect, a sculptor, a teacher. This is the only source of happiness, not money. If you're a professional, you can make enough money to live. Think hard about what you want to do.

You mentioned Rita Levi-Montalcini, a Nobel Prize winner in 1986 for her discovery of growth factors. Do you want to share with us some memories of your friendship with her?

She was a hero by any measure. She grew up in Turin during the time of Benito Mussolini and was kicked out of her country because of anti-Semite laws. She went to the United States with the ideas she'd already developed in Italy. She started to think about how eggs grow and how embryos develop, namely what was the driving force behind differentiation. She went to work in St Louis, and there she met Stanley Cohen, who was working on how the epidermis grows: he was the biochemist and she was the biologist, and together they made astonishing discoveries. Then she came back to Italy and she served as a Senator for Life.

I came to know her obviously late – the difference in age between us is significant – but before she got the Nobel Prize, she, in a way, adopted me. She was fantastic. On top of it all, she was a beautiful lady, always elegant in her jewellery and her dresses. We met many times; she had a profound philosophy about life and I learned a lot from her. I invited her to Israel and she came to visit me. She gave me a very precious gift: her twin sister, Paola, was a gifted painter, but died of a neurodegenerative disease. Therefore, Paola couldn't paint later in her life. Rita gave me one of the last paintings done by Paola Levi-Montalcini. When talking about friendships, I must say that my relationship with Rita was up there at the top throughout my life. She was an unbelievably amazing lady.

An icon and a role model.
I attended her 100th birthday, which was celebrated with a big ceremony in Rome in the Campidoglio, close to the famous statue of Marcus Aurelius. It was wonderful to see this lady getting up and speaking about her ideas, the discoveries she'd made and her contributions to society. She had a 'landscape of life'. Very few people have what I call the 'landscape of life', namely the capacity to look at life from on high and be able to embrace it. And she was one of this kind, no doubt about that.

Professor Edmond Fischer, at the time of her death, Rita Levi-Montalcini was the oldest living Laureate. You won the Nobel Prize in Physiology or Medicine in 1992, and you're currently the oldest living Laureate. What is your memory of Rita?

I met Rita a couple of times in the 1970s to 80s at a meeting or other events. She was considered the Grande Dame of Neuroscience, and everybody looked at her with affection, deep respect and admiration. I got to know her much better when I was invited to come back to Rome to participate in a judging panel at the Accademia dei Lincei for some Italian prize, I don't remember which one. Renato Dulbecco, Rita and I were on the committee with three other Italian life scientists. We gave the prize to Judah Folkman for his pioneering work on angiogenesis. Anyway, on this occasion, I stayed in Rome for several days and had the privilege of spending a lot of time with Rita. She had invited me to give a talk at the Institute of Cell Biology from which she had retired a few years earlier, and she drove me around in her private car with a chauffeur. She took me to a delicious restaurant and to her apartment to meet her twin sister, Paola, a small, seemingly very fragile lady. We chatted in Italian. She was an artist producing mainly modern sculptures. I was amazed that such a frail-looking person could produce works of art of such power and solidity.

I was also amazed that on top of Rita's cluttered desk lay her priceless gold Nobel medal ensconced in a square Plexiglass block. She just laughed when I told her that she must be absolutely crazy, considering the risks of house robberies. I would never do that. Her apartment was very close to the Villa Torlonia, giving on to the Nomentana. In those days, the two large and elegant Mussolini mansions had fallen into a state of total disrepair. But the park was vast, and we went for nice long walks surrounded by a gazillion children. She described at length her war years spent in hiding south of Florence and then about her exciting time with Viktor

Hamburger in St Louis, events well described in her book *In Search of Imperfection*. I asked if she was related to Primo Levi and she said no, but they were very good friends. Primo had died from a fall from the interior landing of his third-storey apartment in Turin. It was reported as a suicide because he had been suffering from bouts of depression, but Rita absolutely refused to accept that he'd taken his own life.

She told me that soon after the excitement and exhilaration of receiving the Nobel Prize, she had real difficulties shouldering the honour and distinctions that people and the Italian Government showered her with. She was given a car with a chauffeur for life, I believe. They built her a new institute and so forth. It got to the point that, within a few months of receiving the award, she became depressed. It was simply more than she was able to deal with.

She gave me a book she'd just published entitled *Il Tuo Futuro* [*Your Future*]. It was devoted to adolescents and their education, mostly to encourage them to make something of their life. Frankly, I thought it was pretty trivial, and doubted the youth of the day would pay much attention to the advice of an old lady, Nobel Laureate or not.

She spoke with great excitement of her new project to create a Magna Carta of Science and wondered what might be the best ways to communicate her thoughts to the scientific community. I suggested she should speak about it at the upcoming Lindau Nobel Laureate Meeting, which she did.[8] I was delighted she went, especially as she'd told me she didn't want to travel anymore so as not to be separated from Paola. Of course, Lindau gave me another opportunity to spend some time with her. She did present her ideas on the Magna Carta at one of the morning plenary lectures, but I think it was received

[8] Available in the Lindau Nobel Mediatheque (www.mediatheque.lindau-nobel.org/)

with only mild interest. I don't believe people paid much attention to her proposal. It was the last time Rita came to Lindau, and the last time I saw her.

Thank you, Professor Fischer! What about the landscape of future discoveries, Professor Ciechanover?
Everybody knows that we've not discovered anything. If you ask me what remains to be discovered, I can reply: everything! We're just scratching at the surface all the time. For example, the brain is still a big mystery. Replacing organs is at its beginning and tissue engineering as well. Gene editing is developing in a big way, with a lot of moral issues. Are we supposed to do it? What should we do with a disease? What is the definition of disease itself? Is being blond a 'disease', if the mother wants the baby to have black hair?

What is ahead of us is not only biology but also a lot of bioethics. We've already started to deal with these aspects and it's truly exciting. We've developed several tools, and we're starting to merge them, which means merging physics into chemistry and into biology. Nature doesn't distinguish between the sciences. Physics is about the particles below atoms that have no names like electrons or whatever, or forces. Chemistry comes from when we started to give names to identify things, like water or hydrogen. Biology is when all these combine to form life, whereas medicine is when something goes wrong in this complex. It's all a continuum. When the Italians invented the first university in the twelfth century in Bologna, they stratified it for the purposes of convenience, but it's an artificial stratification. We're living in an era where we start to go back to the origin and look at nature in a more complex way. We have systems biology and we design molecules in chemistry that will fit into biological structures.

Bridges, not boundaries.
It's the era of unification. Computation will also help us solve big problems. It's about being interdisciplinary: we need

computers to solve problems, structures and interactions. We're at the beginning of this new era.

You can imagine science as an upside-down spiral: we are climbing up, but the spiral becomes wider and wider. Science is endless and discoveries are endless. It's not going to be 'solved'.

But this is the beauty of it. Can you imagine a society where everything is solved, there are no universities and everybody knows everything? It won't happen.

What about the medicine of the future? Are we heading towards 'personalized medicine' or is there more than that? There is more. With personalized medicine, we should be able to diagnose a disease in a patient by also taking into account the genetic mutations. Let's take cancer as an example: the same cancers can have different causes and can be caused by different genetic mutations. Breast cancer, for example, is caused by different mutations. But again, this has ethical implications linked to what we want to know and what we don't want to know. Once we've sequenced the DNA of a patient, we might know more than the patient wants to know, such as the possibility of developing a particular disorder.

There are 'four Ps' for the medicine of the twenty-first century [as described by Leroy Hood]. Personalized is the first. Then predictive: if I can read my DNA, I may be able to predict what I will get. Preventive: if I know what may happen, I may be able to take actions. And participatory: there will be changes in terms of the involvement of the patient, and we will be moving from the patriarchal approach of the old age to a somehow more collaborative effort.

Hopefully avoiding cases where people have read over-whelming information (true and false) on the web and go to the doctor with their own diagnoses ...

But who should store this information? With whom should this information be shared? Are we aware of the issues about the morality of science? Society will have to be safer. It is a big revolution, but science has already dealt with revolutions in the past. We should also take into account the cost of medicine: it will be more expensive. We need to sort the accessibility of medicine: most of the world doesn't have access to these scientific achievements, and we need to think about equality and society, as well as other issues that go well beyond the boundaries of science.

How will universities change?
They will change in many ways, mostly because of interdisciplinary changes: we need to break the boundaries of faculties. We have to make a different 'product' in universities: we need to have physicists with a command of the language of biology and chemistry, and vice versa.

Analysis of datasets to find new waves in this ocean of data that the patients will generate will be crucial, as well as data storage and confidentiality issues. Everything will change. But we're already living in a continuously changing society.

6

Clarity

Tim Hunt

One never notices what has been done;
one can only see what remains to be done.

Marie Curie

Dr Tim Hunt, your father, Richard, was a leading medieval scholar.
Yes, a medievalist.

As a child, were you somehow fascinated by the old manuscripts in your house, and, more generally, by this historical flavour?
The answer is an emphatic 'no'. [He laughs.] I became much more interested later in life. For example, I was in Serbia, and I'd never had any contact with the Eastern Orthodox Church before that. But with the person I was travelling with, when we went into the churches, I was absolutely fascinated to see the differences in style. I've also been in Croatia, just across the border, which is Catholic. The difference between the Catholic and the Orthodox Church is something I'd never focused on before. I discovered that the two Churches split in 1054 in what is called the Great Schism. I became very interested in the doctrine of the Trinity. I discovered that my godfather, who was my dad's best friend and a very distinguished medieval historian, had written a history of the Christian Church covering precisely that period of time. I read this very scholarly account of the history of the Church, the reasons for the split and the differences in doctrines, which are subtle and quite scientific. They have to do with the divinity of Christ and the concept of the Trinity. I couldn't explain them to my grandmother – it was like angels dancing on the head of a pin. Nevertheless, there's a kind of resonation for me with these kinds of things because the scholarship of untangling the evolution of these ideas is not so different from the scholarship of finding out how cells work. I thought it was terrific.

In a way, that was a rediscovery or a revelation.
Exactly. This particularly resonated with me more than for someone who didn't have a medieval historian father. I should say that both my parents were extremely devoted Christians, so I was brought up with concepts such as the

Virgin Birth, although I'm not sure that I really understood the doctrine of the Trinity. The truth is that although I enjoyed Latin quite a lot when I was perhaps seven years old, I gradually found that I was getting worse and worse compared with the other boys. But that was helpful because it turned out that I was rather good at biology, which I learned from a very young age, eleven or twelve. It's an enormous gift to discover that you're worse at something than somebody else, but that you can do something else.

And that, conversely, you have an idea of where you can apply your talents.
Yes. I never had to choose a career path while growing up. I was just drawn to certain stuff.

Let's move from the Middle Ages to modern history and have a brief lesson of the history of science. You made history, and you've crossed paths with people who made it as well.
Yes, I like to say that I've grown up with a sort of 'scientific silver spoon' in my mouth. I've met many Nobel Laureates, and I know a lot of them quite well.

While in Cambridge, you worked, directly or indirectly, with several Nobel Laureates.
Everybody taught me different things, which was very interesting. I would say it began with my real science hero: Francis Crick. He just seemed to be cleverer than anybody else – deeply clever.

Francis Crick, 1962 Nobel Prize winner, along with James Watson, for the discovery of DNA.
He understood everything from the diffraction theory in theoretical physics to the most biological things, and he also ended up studying consciousness. I've never been able to work out whether he actually made a profound contribution to the understanding of consciousness or not.

We will come back to consciousness in one of the following chapters.

In retrospect, Francis Crick was always very kind and considerate; I never had a conversation with him where he wasn't informed about some aspect of my work. The main lesson I learned from him was the importance of clarity. He was in the habit of attending practically every seminar – or at least every interesting one – whatever the topic. He would come to the seminars, sit at the back and often ask questions that, it was clear, were aimed at clarifying things, not showing how clever he was. Some of the others would ask nasty questions to show how clever they were and how stupid the speaker was, but not Francis. And that was terrific.

There was a period in my life when he used to have lunch in the tearoom of the Laboratory of Molecular Biology. He would come and sit down, and would explain what he was doing and what he was thinking about. He was always very careful to involve everybody around the table, and to make sure that everyone was up to speed and to clarify things. That was fantastic. I admired him for that. The other thing was the sheer heterogeneity of the great scientists in a way that was incredibly encouraging, because you realized that there wasn't a given path. If you'd met Fred Sanger without knowing who he was, you would have taken him for the gardener or the janitor. He was a very quiet, softly spoken, modest person.

Fred Sanger won the Prize in Chemistry in 1958 'for his work on the structure of proteins, especially that of insulin'.[9]
I discovered that Fred Sanger had been very kind to me and influenced my getting my postdoctoral fellowship, a crucial juncture in my life. It was clear that these people quietly operated in the background by taking care of people they thought were worth taking care of.

---

[9] www.nobelprize.org

What about Sydney Brenner, one of the 2002 Nobel Prize recipients in Physiology or Medicine for his 'discoveries concerning genetic regulation of organ development and programmed cell death'?[9]

With Sydney, it was special. He used to be scary. I got to know Sydney better very recently. He was the founding President of the Okinawa Institute of Science and Technology (OIST), where my wife got a job. Sydney set it up. I've seen him in operation, and it's very interesting. He was a great pioneer who first understood the need for the existence of messenger RNA, which was a real paradigm shift. He was extraordinary and his knowledge was comprehensive: an absolutely brilliant lecturer. However, as biochemistry students, we were forbidden from going to that course on the strange grounds that we already had enough stuff to do. But it was because some people hated Sydney, and Sydney hated them. And that was OK.

And what about Max Perutz, the 1962 co-winner in Chemistry for his 'studies of the structures of globular proteins'?[9]

In line with this, someone once reminded me of this story: Max Perutz gave lectures on the structure of globular proteins in, I suppose, the 1950s. These lectures were extremely well attended and used to take place in a rather obscure place. Finally, to Max's delight, he was invited to transfer the location of his lectures from this obscure location to the biochemistry department. However, when he came to give the lectures, nobody showed up.

I can't believe this.

And the reason was, again, that the biochemistry students were told they shouldn't go there. There was a tremendous amount of friction between the biochemistry and the molecular chemistry departments! Outrageous, absolutely outrageous, and very sort of funny and silly.

How was Max Perutz as a person and lecturer?

Max was a complicated person. He fancied himself, but he didn't want to appear pleased with himself. He used to give these lectures, which took place at five o'clock in the evening. He turned the lights off and got his assistants to bring him down a model of haemoglobin. He would lecture while handling an electric torch in the dark to highlight particular residues and sites. At five o'clock, at the end of a long, hard day, it could become boring and incomprehensible – and I must admit that I tended to fall asleep. But, having said that, he was a brilliant Director of the Laboratory of Molecular Biology, and he selected terrific people to work with. I remember that one day a friend who worked for a friend of mine gave a wonderful talk at the annual lab talks. After the talk, I congratulated the speaker and said: 'That was a wonderful talk!' Max was standing nearby and said: 'No, it was wonderful science' [he imitates the voice]. In some ways, he was one of my heroes.

What about César Milstein? He won the Nobel Prize in Physiology or Medicine in 1984 for 'theories concerning the specificity in development and control of the immune system and the discovery of the principle for production of monoclonal antibodies'.[9]

César was great. I really liked him. He was just extraordinary. Unfortunately, he died before his time.

Have we forgotten someone?

Of course, there was the next generation of people, my generation, many of whom you might know quite well: Roger Kornberg, Martin Chalfie, Andy Fire, John Sulston.

We'll meet Martin Chalfie in the next chapter.

I don't think we would have seen ourselves remotely in the same league as our boyhood heroes Watson and Crick and the others.

But now you are in the same league.

It turns out that it was pretty straightforward. We'd been working on exciting things. We talked to each other. Sometimes we could help each other and sometimes not. We were very interested, and it was a matter of working hard to find things out, putting one foot in front of the other. Science isn't rocket science: it's very simple. It's about doing the assay, measuring things, doing the right controls, and sometimes you stumble into something interesting. Most often, you don't, as things usually don't work very well. It's depressing as hell, but that's OK. It would never have occurred to me that we would become 'tomorrow's Nobel Laureates'. But actually we were, and we are. It goes back to the aforementioned matter of clarity. Just keep it simple: our brain is only this big, and if you try to be too clever, you'll walk around with your head in the clouds without looking where you are going.

At the beginning of your career, one event could have led to something terrible but, instead, it was an unexpectedly fortunate (re-)starting point. In 1974, your laboratory was destroyed by a fire. You had to move to a new space, and Max Perutz helped you in that situation. How was restarting from zero, from a *tabula rasa*?
It was absolutely great.

How did you turn an unfortunate event into something good?
Well, that's how it was. I got a phone call at about seven a.m. on a Saturday morning. I was reached by my colleague, Richard Jackson: 'Tim, the lab has burned down. Don't bother to come in because nothing's left.' Indeed, I went and I found that some precious samples could still be saved, but everything else was burned. We lost every note and a paper we were working on. At that time, we'd been struggling to understand what we were working on, so it was just great that the notebooks were destroyed: it was like making a confession in church. Most of the equipment was old and rusty. We then set up a lovely new lab with new equipment in a new place with some wonderful colleagues. Max said that we could have lunch in the tearoom and I became very friendly with many of the people working there. It was like a breath of fresh air. Also, it was slightly removed from the stultifying atmosphere

of the biochemistry department. The stores were very good in the molecular biology section too. We used to have supper at the hospital canteen, which was a great meeting place. Never underestimate the importance of information exchange, even that occurring in a smoking club or other random interactions.

Breakthroughs are often first hailed with scepticism and criticism. You won the Nobel Prize in Physiology or Medicine in 2001, with Leland Hartwell and Sir Paul Nurse, for your experiments on 'key regulators of the cell cycle'.[9] How did the people around you act when you made your Nobel discovery?
They were very sceptical. But I knew in my heart and bones that I'd just made an incredibly important and exciting discovery.

And then your telephone rang for the Nobel call.
That was great news, but very hard to take.

Why do you say that?
Because the early development of the field had been a very nice collaboration with many people I like, admire and respect. Paul Nurse and Lee Hartwell won on the genetics side, but on the physiological and biochemical side, there were a number of possible people – I'm just lucky that I made it.

Lucky?
I was a good example of what Pasteur said: 'Chances favour the prepared mind.' I think my mind had been exceedingly well prepared. I'm well aware I'm not as clever or as talented – I was lucky. Maybe what I emphasized earlier on, namely the clarity training that Cambridge provided me with, was very helpful – trying to keep it simple.

Trying to keep it simple is a piece of golden advice for future generations of scientists.
I think so. I recognized that when I was much younger. We had all these role models, and they were incredibly clever. We tried

to be very clever too, but we weren't clever enough to keep it simple. By the time you get three or four different factors interacting, it's already difficult. I'm deeply suspicious of a lot of what passes for systems biology today: people think that, by measuring absolutely everything, the truth will emerge as a sort of phoenix, and the whole will be clear. But this isn't how it works. Science is like walking into a foggy landscape. You can't make anything out clearly. When the fog lifts, you can see a tree here and a bush there, and it becomes obvious which way to go. But the fog always descends again. It's about this moment of clarity that is treasurable, and it comes along every, let's say, ten years or something like that.

Clarity can guide us through the fog.
In my experience, guessing ahead of time how something works is incredibly difficult. Then, when you see it, you ask yourself what took you so long. In retrospect, the solution was obvious – a kind of inevitability.

But only in retrospect?
Yes, only retrospectively. This is something I heard Francis Crick saying once: there are always so many possibilities in biology that choosing which one Nature has decided to evolve is not easy. It'll be extremely interesting to see maybe in five or ten years or 100 or 1000: will the secrets, for example, of how the brain thinks be revealed to us? I don't know and it's impossible to say – like for the discovery of place cells in the brain.

A discovery that was awarded the Nobel Prize in 2014. I was in Stockholm and attended the Nobel Lectures, which were focused on the 'GPS of the brain'.
Gosh, so we do have a map inside! Wow! However, we still don't have a clue how to interrogate these maps. Let's come back again to Sydney Brenner. He studied the brain of a nematode because he thought that genetics plus the neuro-anatomy of these worms could tell us a lot about it, and he

published a paper entitled 'The mind of a worm.' But he didn't understand the mind of a worm, and even if we do get to understand it, it still wouldn't predict how the worm's brain is wired and the relations between the brain and behaviour. So interesting!

We can't predict the scientific future.

Where the next breakthrough will come from is totally unpredictable and unknowable, and it's important to make that point. We know what we'd like to know. For example, I would love to know how the brain thinks: it would be great, but we don't know. Switching analogy, the research I've been doing is like turning over stones and seeing what's underneath. Most of them just have sand or dirt, but every so often there's something interesting there. The whole point is you don't know what you're going to find. Only in retrospect can you say, 'Ah, of course, it has to be like that!' But it didn't have to be like that. There are millions of ways of explaining it. People who claim that you can predict the future don't understand what they're up against. And, in biology, you're constantly surprised.

And that's also part of the beauty of science.

And that's the beauty of science. But there is a big 'but', and it's what I call the ambassador's problem. I once gave a talk in front of the British ambassador to Thailand, very charming but not a scientist. He told me, 'It was a lovely talk, but I didn't really understand any of it.' Pierre-Gilles de Gennes, a French physicist who won the Nobel Prize for his work on liquid viscose, wrote a book entitled *Soft Interfaces*. At the end, he wrote some notes on style. There, he wrote about the difficulty of explaining beautiful scientific ideas. He said that something like music – let's say a flute player in Bogotá – can immediately be approached and grasped. It's beautiful, and everybody responds to that. In contrast, beautiful ideas in science are sometimes only accessible to people who have shared a long training in that particular science. Sometimes, beautiful ideas in science aren't even accessible to scientists from other fields, because, to fully understand it, you need a huge amount of background that could take years to acquire.

That's the problem of explaining science.
I like to give the example that occurred to me when my then seven-year-old daughter asked me, 'Daddy, why is the ceiling opaque?' You look at the ceiling and the light doesn't get through the ceiling. Then you look at the glass in the window, and it's as solid as the ceiling, but the light comes straight through. What's going on? To appreciate it, you have to understand quantum theory rather deeply, and I don't. I know it's beyond me mathematically to deal with it. During the luncheon given by the British Ambassador in Stockholm, I asked Aaron Klug, the Nobel Laureate, how the light gets through. He told me that I first needed to understand the Schrödinger equation. I looked up at what the Schrödinger equation was, and it starts with the square root of minus one, which I remember being my nemesis in maths. Even if I could understand the concept, I can't manipulate it. The fact is that light gets through the glass, but I don't understand why it gets through the glass and not through the wall.

What was your reply to your daughter?
Her question set me on a quest trying to find out myself. Nobody ever explained these things to us at school, and we just took them for granted. I've discovered that asking this kind of question leads you to very beautiful concepts that are deep and interesting. Physics is difficult, because if you're not good at maths, it's all over, so it's certainly beyond me. Biology was easier because the concepts aren't nearly so difficult. However, I'll tell you another story about this. I was in Singapore for a sort of Nobel Laureates meeting, and I came across Anthony Leggett.

Anthony J. Leggett won the Nobel Prize for discovering the properties of helium-3, a theoretical quantum mechanics explanation.

His story is fascinating: it turned out that he'd never done any science at school or at university. He studied Latin and Greek, history and philosophy, literature and language. It wasn't until he started worrying about what to do next that he thought philosophy might be the thing. He then realized that philosophical theories are rather arbitrary. He decided that physics would be the closest approach to experimental philosophy. The problem was how to switch from Greek and Latin to theoretical physics. You should read his Nobel Lecture – it's fascinating.

I will!

He should have gone on military service because he was eligible. But what happened – what saved him – was that the Russians launched Sputnik, and suddenly the nation decided that they needed physicists. He was a very bright young man: it's true that he only knew Latin, Greek and a bit of philosophy, but he'd done some extra maths at school because of a visiting teacher, and this helped him. They accepted him to do accelerated physics in Oxford for a two-year course, which he managed, and the rest is history. He's always had a gift for language. This is just wonderful: you don't need to do science. Maybe science shouldn't be a school subject? Although I'm glad it was and I did it. That's the story.

A scientist's life is also about dealing with frustration. What has been the most difficult period of your life and how did you get through it?

There were long periods when I thought I'd never make a discovery. Finding a good problem is difficult. My great schoolboy hero, the Nobel Laureate Peter Medawar, wrote beautiful essays and a book entitled *Memoir of a Thinking Radish*. He also wrote an essay entitled *The Art of the Soluble*, where he talks about this. He wrote that scientists are not remembered because they *tackled* difficult problems but because they *solved* interesting problems. Finding a problem that's both interesting and soluble is the name of the game. It's not easy: you never know, at a given moment, whether you can solve the problem. In my experience, it can take around five to ten years to solve a good problem. It should be a difficult problem, because if it's too easy, someone else will solve it before you do. Once again, the fire in the lab helped me to better focus on the problem to study. When things go badly, and they usually go badly, you don't know if other people are doing better than you and you're stuck with something; you just keep going. In my case, for example, I wouldn't have known what to do otherwise.

I'm very sorry for what happened in July 2015. [Dear reader, all is online, and the details have already been clarified.]
Well, that was a very unpleasant situation and extremely debilitating and puzzling. What can I say? I was a silly boy.

You've mentioned many books during our conversation. Are you an avid reader?
I've recently come across a book by a mathematician called Cédric Villani.

He was awarded the 2010 Fields Medal.
The book is called *Birth of a Theorem*. Again, I met him in Singapore. I like books on the history of science.

I love the history of science.
One can learn a lot from the history of science. You learn a lot from heroes. It's perhaps not very fashionable, but I've always found it inspiring. The first book I ever read was the biography of Madame Curie, which I found extremely inspiring. I love the history of quantum mechanics: it was so difficult, and it took so long. Schrödinger, Heisenberg, Dirac, Pauli and Tomonaga: what great pioneers, how extremely amazing. Sometimes I got the chance to hear directly from some of these key players in the history of science. In Okinawa, in Japan, I was a member

of the Board of Governors, and the members were interesting people. Once I was in a cab with Jerome Isaac Friedman. I asked him, 'Jerry, what did you win the Nobel Prize for?' And he replied, 'Well, I guess you can say that my group provided the first experimental evidence for the existence of quarks.' And my reaction was, 'Wow! How did you discover quarks?' And then he told me the full story, in the back of the cab!

Fascinating. Great stories, great people.
I know these people. They're pretty ordinary human beings, maybe eccentric in some ways and perfectly ordinary in other ways, and they figured out things that we didn't know before their work, thus realizing fantastic breakthroughs in understanding. It's just wonderful. A lot of that wonder and of the extraordinary is also something good that has to do with the education I had in Cambridge, because we were used to wondering and asking questions. How do we know this? What are the next experiments? How are we going to find out the next steps? We were constantly probing away at nature. It's a noble activity and a romantic one. It's all about the quest for the truth, values, rigorous self-examination, honesty. Nature is constantly telling you, 'You got things wrong.' I like to say that nature is always biting you on the ankles. You know when things are going right, but when they're going wrong, it's like you're having a dialogue with nature. Sometimes it seems like nature says, 'Well, yes. So what?'

It looks like a challenge with nature: a noble activity and, sometimes, a Nobel one.
It's been good fun. And it's been good fun because of the people you work with.

A collaborative effort indeed.
Yes, with friends and also rivals.

7

Mentoring

Martin Chalfie, Hamilton O. Smith and Johann Deisenhofer

I have created nothing really beautiful, really lasting, but if I can inspire one of these youngsters to develop the talent I know they possess, then my monument will be in their work.

Augusta Savage

Professor Martin Chalfie, when we first met in 2010, your lecture was introduced by your mentor, Robert Perlman. What do having a mentor and becoming a mentor mean?

That's a beautiful question. I've recently thought about who my mentors have been. I think there's a whole series of people, not just one person. You often hear stories where one person does everything and changes someone's life, but I've been mentored or helped by a great number of people. Certainly my parents: they gave me a lot of freedom and many interests, but they weren't academic people. They grew up during the Depression. I don't believe my father finished high school, and my mother had to leave college because she couldn't pay the tuition. Yet they were very supportive. I never got the feeling that they were anything other than exceptionally happy about what I was doing and that I had this interest in science.

Their support was very good. I'll tell you one story. My father was a professional guitarist. I was the oldest of his three sons, and one day, probably when I was twelve or so, he gave me a guitar. My father had a very interesting way of teaching the guitar, and I'll remember this forever. He never said to me, 'That's not the way to do it – do it this way!' He was a professional, and he knew how to do it. He would show me how to do things, but he never said I was doing things incorrectly. I've always been somehow amazed by this sort of support. He was genuinely supportive of my learning about something he wanted me to learn, but without telling me what to do. I wish I'd learned that lesson better!

In terms of science mentors, there are different aspects, not only people who showed you how to be a good scientist but also those showing you real humanity. For example, when I first started college, I took a second-year calculus course, my first class in college. At the beginning of the course, the tutor said, 'There's no textbook for the class, but I have a lot of notes that I wrote during the summer in a cafe in Paris.' I said to myself, 'That's what I want to do!' That was so fascinating.

Then there were other influential people, in much more meaningful ways. For example, in college, I took a course in cell physiology from an incredible scientist, Woody Hastings, who'd been working on bioluminescence and who died some years ago. He was in charge of this course, but, unfortunately, I couldn't go to the library during its regular opening hours because of other obligations. I needed a key to go to the biology library and get the books to study for the course. I went to his office, which was on the fourth floor, whereas the library was on the ground floor. I told him I needed a key and the reasons behind my request. He said yes, and I thought he would simply write a note that I could have taken down with me. But he didn't. He got up from behind his desk and said, 'Come with me.' He walked down the four floors of stairs to the library office and said, 'This guy needs a key. Please give it to him.' This extra effort, not seen in my other professors, made a very big impression on me.

Other people were very important through their work and made a significant contribution, such as Joel Rosenbaum and Ron Morris. I met them in Cambridge, and we usually had wonderful conversations. One day, out of the blue, both of them at a different time said, 'If you need a letter of recommendation, I'll be happy to write it for you.' That was a very important lesson: the wonderful scientists are those who help people because they're excited about the work they're doing. That was very, very nice.

What about Robert Perlman, with you on stage during the first lecture of yours I attended?
Bob Perlman was the perfect PhD adviser for me. I was quite naive and very unsure of myself. I'd taken three years between college and graduate school. I'd worked in a lab just before going to graduate school, and there I got my first publication, so I had a bit of confidence, but I was just starting out. Fortunately for me, I was assigned a desk in Bob Perlman's lab, right outside his office. Bob almost always had his door

open. I felt absolutely comfortable talking with him about any stupid or crazy idea I had. I brought to him whatever weird idea impressed and interested me at the time. Being able to have someone who gave his time was wonderful. He's an exceptionally wonderful person to work with: even the frustrating parts were a lot of fun. Bob was definitely one of my most important mentors. Things changed when I did my postdoc because my adviser was Sydney Brenner at the Laboratory of Molecular Biology (LBM) in Cambridge. And Sydney was very different from Bob.

We've talked a little bit about Nobel Prize winner Sydney Brenner with Tim Hunt, and you were in Cambridge at the same time.

Sydney was doing his own research, and he was accepting people as postdocs. It was understood, from the very first second, that you were on your own, a kind of 'independent contractor' working on whatever you chose, not on his project. And going to the LMB (Laboratory of Molecular Biology) was both eye-opening and an unbelievably wonderful part of the story. There were astonishing scientists and amazing colleagues, and I learned from all of them. They were all my mentors. There was every piece of equipment you could ever have wanted, or they could make it for you. And there was almost every supply you needed. Everything was available. This was both wonderful and scary: I suddenly realized I was the person who had to make the decisions – the particular work to do, when the paper should be ready, and everything else. Many at the laboratory were flourishing in that period, but some people found it very difficult: it wasn't the best thing for everybody. But for me, having people like John White and John Sulston, Jonathan Hodgkin, Bob Horvitz and others who were my companions (we were a group of fourteen people), all interacting with each other, was fantastic. Everyone was everybody else's mentor, and I had much to learn. It was exciting to be part of the tradition of really good science. You had to step up your game to be part of it. That was important and, as I said, exciting.

Sydney was my mentor, but he mentored me by leaving me to my own devices. It was funny to look at the 2002 Nobel Prize winners in Medicine and Physiology, because all three had an exceptionally important role in my life. Sydney gave me this incredible opportunity and was very supportive, even though I only talked to him about science maybe once a year for the five years I was there. John Sulston was the person I had done most work with. The project he'd originally started, before he decided to go off to do other things, had been left; it was to look at touch sensitivity and for mutants defective for touch. And it was Bob Horvitz who, just before I arrived in Cambridge, told me, 'John Sulston has this wonderful set of mutants that he's not going to be working with. You might consider taking over the project.' It was quite nice! One final comment about John Sulston: he's not only the greatest experimentalist I've ever met, but also one of the most moral people. He set a level about how one should communicate, how one should be as a person doing science, more than anything else: that had a very strong effect on me. John is an absolutely wonderful person and has done several things to help many people, and I'm one of the recipients of his kindness.

Then, there is a final set of mentors, and they're the people who work in my lab. I have learned as much from them as they've learned from me. The very best interactions in the lab aren't between mentors and students and postdocs, but among colleagues. You get to a point when people are interacting with each other, when everyone is contributing, and there's no ego. I've been very fortunate in having many friends with whom, after a very short time, I can just discuss the work, rather than 'I have to do this for my thesis' or 'I am worried about this.' What has amazed me about the best of the colleagues in the lab is that, if they see the sense of a suggestion (and we hotly debate ideas), no matter who has made it, they just say, 'Yeah,

I'll do that' – and they're gone. We work together, and that's so much fun. I've learned from them as well. And I've also learned a lot from my wife and daughter. You learn from a lot of people, and it is the interaction, I think, that's the truly wonderful thing.

The transitions from graduate student to university professor often imply going through a postdoctoral period. To get a postdoc, you need to contact a researcher and write a solid application. When we met in Lindau in 2014, I remember that you gave many pieces of advice on how to craft a postdoc application.

This is one of my campaigns. I believe that ninety-nine per cent of postdoc applications are done incorrectly. My little campaign tries to convince as many students as possible, and to tell them to tell their friends, although I'm not sure if this always works.

This is how I believe people should apply. Most applications I've seen over more than thirty years at Columbia read something like this: 'Dear Professor, I am interested in doing a postdoc in your lab.' It starts with some nice sentences or compliments, such as 'I like your work', and then 'I am attaching my CV and here are the names of three people who can write on my behalf.' And they send it off. Of course, this letter can be sent to hundreds or even thousands of people. There is nothing in it at all. My point is that graduate students, when they graduate, shouldn't do another stint as graduate students. Instead, they should become colleagues. This puts an entirely different twist on the application, because if you're coming as a colleague, you should already have some ideas about what you want to do. I tell people that in the application they should write something like: 'I have been reading and thinking about your work and I have developed a two- or three-page proposal of the work that I would like to do in your laboratory.' This proposal, among other things, shows the person who might hire you how you think, how excited you are about it, and it allows the applicant to get excited about coming as a colleague. More than that, this is your idea, something you have developed. I want to see the excitement that potential postdocs will bring. I want them to be committed to the project. If they think it's their project, as it will be, they'll be all set.

A couple more things you can write: 'You may also have some unpublished work, and I would be happy to think about that too', not 'I would be happy to do that' because the student is not coming to the laboratory as a technician or in a subservient position – this shows they can come up with their own ideas. After that, I would like to ban the line saying, 'Here are the names of three people who can write on my behalf.' I think it's a horrible thing. If you want to be hired by a store, would you walk into the store and say, 'I want to work here. Here is what you have to do to hire me'? A student can instead write something like, 'These are the names of three people whom I have asked to write a letter to you. If you do not get these letters in the next three days, please let me know.' You can add: 'I have looked at the fellowships I would be eligible for. I am going to this meeting, and if you are going to be there, I would love to talk to you. Is there a chance we can meet there or would you like to arrange a Skype meeting?' Anything that shows that the person is taking charge of their career is welcome. This way, the students see the mentor as an important step in their goal, not just a person to work with because their laboratory is a good place to work.

Thanks for this! I know you're a swimmer.
Not recently. I used to be a swimmer. And I should still be a swimmer.

You were the captain of the Harvard swimming team and, in your freshman year, undefeated in the 100-yard fly.
I don't even remember that!

I read this in *The Harvard Crimson*.
I'd love to read the article – that's terrific! But I'm not so sure it means anything. The reason is that the distance we were swimming during competitions – and I can tell you that I didn't win all the time – was 200 yards, not 100 yards. So I might have been undefeated at 100 yards because we didn't swim it in competitions! I honestly don't remember. I was an OK swimmer. I enjoyed swimming and the friendships being on the team enabled.

Colleges are strange places, at least here in the United States, because they represent a very big transition. I like to say that one might already have brothers and sisters, but then you go and make new relationships with roommates and new friends in college. You have people who go to class with you, and this won't happen later in life. You're an adult. However, unless you do something, colleges can be fairly lonely places. Roommates help, but what helped me was having the sort of friends I saw every day: the people of the swimming team. That was a sort of island of stability. The lab can also be such an island. Because it's exactly the same thing: you don't have to be part of a swimming team or an *a cappella* choir or theatrical production: you can work in a lab and the people in the lab become friends. This provides stability and a sort of grounding that I think is essential.

What's more difficult: leading a swimming team to victory or a lab to great results?
I've never felt that I was leading a team to victory. It was nice that my fellow team members voted for me to be team captain in my senior year – maybe most of the seniors had dropped out of the team by then and I was the only one who stayed around! [He laughs.] It was nice to be part of that group. I was captain for one season only and head of the lab for longer.

A very important thing is that people need individual attention. Some people need this attention in the same way Sydney gave me, namely by letting me do whatever I wanted. In my lab, I've had people who were creative and self-motivated, whereas others I probably should have talked to more. I'm a bit of a hands-off person: I love talking about the work, but I don't enjoy the individual troubleshooting much – talking about a particular experiment. I like taking an overview and talking about that. When people in my laboratory finally get to the point of writing up the work, it's the beginning: they have to look at the results and think about what they mean and how to interpret them. However, it's often the case that the paper has outlined a story with a conclusion; but while looking at all the data, we find there's another story we hadn't anticipated. This has happened numerous times in the lab. This is not perhaps the greatest model for doing science – I'm not sure I'm a model for this – but having some data can lead us to pose questions that we didn't have before.

There's a problem here, and I'm not sure that I've addressed it as I should have. When you have a person who is doing well, whose experiments are often working and who is producing lots of data, while writing the paper there's also a learning process on how to write the paper itself and how to put things together. But, for some people, this isn't easy, and their experiments may not be going well. Although I talk to people once a week individually and during lab meetings, those meetings and conversations are all about the immediate situation and the immediate problems. I realized that for people having trouble, and who are not used to regularly writing a paper, we only had individual momentary discussions. The people working on papers more often had a totally different perspective because we usually talked about the whole project and how the parts fit together. I realized that the first group of people weren't getting enough attention. I tried to get around that by suggesting to people that, if they had anything to write at any time, they should start writing a paper about what they've done so far to get an overview, a broader look at what they're doing. I'm not sure if this is working as there's a certain resistance sometimes to this approach. I do let people be very independent.

But sometimes experiments don't work …
I often have graduate students and postdocs asking me how I cope with frustration when experiments aren't working. A Principal Investigator often works with a number of people, and if one person's experiments are working, they feel good and are less upset about those that aren't working. That's why a good way of approaching science is doing more than one thing at the same time. If you have more than one project, when you get bored with one thing, you have another one to work on.

You won the Nobel Prize in Chemistry for 'the discovery and development of the green fluorescent protein, GFP'. Before the final submission, something stood between your Nobel manuscript and its publication: your wife. A final experiment was missing, and she was the person in charge of it. She posed three conditions for the data to be shared with you (and, therefore, for the manuscript to be submitted): '(1) you make coffee every Saturday morning for the next two months, ready by 8.30 a.m.; (2) you prepare a special French dinner at a time of your choosing; and (3) you empty the garbage nightly for the next month'.[10] Conditions (1) and (3) had a deadline, but the second one didn't. Did the French dinner ever take place?
She claims that I've never paid up any of the three conditions, and that I still owe these, periodically. It is a very funny thing: the conditions are included in the letter that I showed during my Nobel Lecture. I often joke about this terrific letter. It represents not only something humorous but also allows me to talk about the important work that my wife did. She did her work entirely on her own. What we did in our 1994 *Science*

[10] www.nobelprize.org

paper was to show that one can take the controlling elements of the gene and use them to express GFP, so we could see where, when and how much of the protein was made. My wife's experiment was the next important step: she took an entire gene, the controlling region and the coding region, and then fused the coding region to GFP. She made the first protein fusion: she could watch the protein moving, and that was a tremendously important experiment.

The Nobel Prize can't be assigned to more than three people. When your award was announced in 2008 (shared with Osamu Shimomura and Roger Y. Tsien), Douglas C. Prasher, who conducted his research on the *Aequorea victoria* jellyfish in the early 1990s, didn't receive the Nobel Prize. You have always acknowledged his remarkable contribution and have been defined as a science gentleman for this. Now, apparently, he drives a courtesy van for a car dealer in Huntsville.

Douglas was always a collaborator. He was the last author of our 1994 *Science* paper, and I think a middle author in a paper by Roger Tsien too. Without his contribution, the experiments would have been impossible. Douglas was exceptionally important for the work. He also, independently, had the idea that GFP could be a marker. The problem with the Nobel is that it only goes to three people. That's the issue.

Is it time for the Nobel Prize to extend the limit of three winners per year per category?

It must be a horrible thing to go through the nominations trying to decide the three people who should be awarded the Prize. It's easy for the people who are asked to nominate someone, but making the decision must be horrible. I'm very glad I don't have anything to do with that. I like to say that the GFP story can be divided in a number of different ways. I have a friend in the department whom I was talking with some months after I won the Nobel. Knowing that he thought my wife's work was very important, I asked him if he believed that the wrong member of my family got the Prize. He looked at me and said, 'You're right!' I was very fortunate to be considered one of the three people to receive the Nobel. I'm very happy about it and I'm not giving it back!

Professor Hamilton Smith, Nobel Prize winner in Physiology or Medicine in 1978 and Professor Johann Deisenhofer, who won the Nobel Prize in Chemistry in 1988, will join us for some questions. Is it time to change the three-people rule?
Chalfie: It's probably a good idea to keep it as it is. The Peace Prize has sometimes been given to an organization, and, for certain things, an organization might be a better way. I don't have an opinion either way, but I can see how difficult these decisions are. I know that the Nobel people don't want to change it. This is their decision.

Smith: Generally, I would say no. It's so highly recognized in part because it is so exclusive.

Deisenhofer: No. This is hard for me to imagine.

Maybe, in the future, there will be a university or a group of universities winning the Prize for a shared discovery?
Chalfie: There are other things to think about here. One of the projects I was quite intrigued by was the cloning of the Huntington's disease gene, supported in large part by the Hereditary Disease Foundation. The model was this: we have money and we'll give it to you, but there are two conditions. If you want it, you have to come to a meeting twice a year with all the other people getting our money, and you have to tell them everything about your research progress. Second, whichever lab clones the gene, everyone will be on the paper: it will be the 'Huntington Consortium' because it's been a joint project, and that's because we've given you the money. And it worked! The same thing happened with the first gene identified as the basis of amyotrophic lateral sclerosis. Those sorts of efforts are quite wonderful ways of getting things done and of structuring things so that people cooperate more. As I mentioned earlier, John Sulston structured the *C. elegans* genome project so that

everyone had to share their data for publication, and we all benefited from it. There are some times in science when things can be structured: you know exactly where you're going in terms of experimental questions. Other times, it's about large groups trying to answer these questions. But often there are a couple of key people who had the ideas that started it, and I'm not so sure that they couldn't be recognized. In conclusion, I can see both possibilities.

Smith: That could be okay. A team could be honoured as a group for a discovery that they all shared in.

Deisenhofer: This is hard for me to imagine.

Professor Chalfie, you won the Nobel Prize, but I think you missed the Nobel call.
Chalfie: Yes, I did. I slept through it, because my wife and I live in an apartment and we have a single telephone in our kitchen, and our bedrooms have two doors that were closed between ourselves and the phone. Also, inadvertently, the day before, I'd pressed some wrong buttons and the ring tone was much softer. I found out that I'd won the Nobel by going on the website and looking to see who'd won that day.

What were you doing when your telephone rang for the Nobel call, Professor Smith?
Smith: It was about 8.30 a.m. and I was headed to the door to drive down to Hopkins to teach 100 medical students when the call came. It was the Associated Press. They told me the news and wanted an interview. It was totally unexpected, but, for some reason, I didn't think it was a prank. Nowadays, you hear from the Nobel Committee first, but at that time, the press called first. My mouth went dry and I asked them to call back in ten minutes. My wife saw me answer the call and wanted to know what it was. Meanwhile, another reporter called, and I did a brief interview. When I finally got out the door and drove to Hopkins, the news had broken, so Dan Nathans, who shared the Prize, called off the lecture.

What about you, Professor Deisenhofer?
Deisenhofer: The phone call came during my morning shower. For some reason, I stepped out of the shower and answered it.

Thank you, Professor Deisenhofer and Professor Smith. Professor Chalfie, GFP has been widely applied in many different areas, ranging from detecting landmines to crafting a 'green beer' for St Patrick's Day. What is the future of GFP?
The thing that's amazing about GFP-related research, to me, is that it has taken so many different new directions, and almost all of these have been things that I'd have never imagined. There were things that I did imagine, such as mutating GFP to get different colours beyond 'green'. What I didn't realize was that there would be other organisms with significantly different fluorescence proteins. We're finding a large number of organisms with these fluorescence proteins. I don't know where it's going to go and what sort of things are going to be done, but we have opened up the box, in a sense. People have found astonishing proteins. Every year somebody comes up with new ideas for GFP and it's quite wonderful.

Your story shows that applications and 'translations' of discoveries to other fields of study are possible thanks to basic research.
The main point I'd like to make about the story of the discovery of GFP is that it started with Osamu Shimomura's work. He discovered the *Aequorea victoria* jellyfish, calcium indicator and GFP. This produced a wonderful tool, but it came from studying a jellyfish, and from exploring a process that has nothing at all to do with any real applications that one can imagine until you start thinking about it – and that is bioluminescence.

Unbelievable discoveries that have many applications, ultimately for human health, come from works that have nothing to do with human health, by studying fascinating biological problems. This is a bit of a lesson. On the one hand, one can say that we should be looking more at life because there's so much more to learn. But time after time, the breakthroughs allowing translational or applied works come from advances in fundamental research. To me, it's a balance. I like to make a joke at seminars that, as I'm getting older, I want to see more translational works on the diseases I'm going to get. But, in reality, I know that basic research is the foundation for subsequent treatments, preventive measures and general improvements in medicine.

Many discoveries didn't start with something like: 'I am going to cure a disease', but rather by exploiting the underpinning biological background information. I don't label *C. elegans*, *Drosophila* and mice as 'model organisms' because I don't like this term. What 'model organism' says is that we're modelling something that will be like humans, and I don't think this is the right term. Instead – and I don't know if I've heard this term from somebody else – I prefer using 'pioneer organism': we learn something new about biology from them. What we find is more or less universal: it's a piece that has been missing because perhaps people were looking too closely at it. By looking a little further afield, people sometimes find things that are much more general and much more important.

8

A Stroke
of Colour

Roger Y. Tsien

I draw from Nature, although in completely new terms.

Bridget Riley

'If you could choose an object that has mattered a lot to you, your work or creative process, what would it be?' Each Nobel Laureate is asked this question, and to bring this object and donate it to the Nobel Museum when coming to Stockholm to receive their Prize. Professor Roger Tsien, what object did you choose and what memories are linked to that object?

I gave a small notebook containing assorted jottings from childhood, aged about eight to thirteen, in which I had drawn imaginary streets and expressway maps, some Chinese lessons, notes from chemistry experiments, etc. I'd forgotten that I'd even kept such a notebook until the Nobel Museum requested a gift, which made me rummage through an old trunk my parents had filled with my childhood leftovers.

Aged sixteen, you won the prestigious Westinghouse Science Talent Search, a nationwide science competition. The senior judge was the Nobel Laureate Glenn Seaborg. What do you remember of that experience and, specifically, of Professor Seaborg?

He was much taller than me, and intimidating because he was an inorganic chemist and thus an expert in the field of my project.

Your father, uncles and brothers developed a family tradition of engineering studies, and you somehow renovated this tradition by 'using chemistry to build biologically useful molecules'.[11] However, beyond the breakthrough and the technical relevance of green fluorescent protein for which you won the Nobel Prize in Chemistry in 2008, together with Osamu Shimomura and Martin Chalfie, the artistic beauty of these images is stunning. You love science, but what about art?

I was intrigued by art and took various undergraduate art history and visual studies classes. I respond most strongly to painters who use bold colours, like Giuseppe Arcimboldo, Henri Matisse, Yaacov Agam, Bridget Riley and David

---

[11] www.nobelprize.org

Hockney. I've often said that it's important in science to pick projects that give one some sensual pleasure, which in my case means pretty – even gaudy – colours. In my first successful science experiments, calcium imaging, the rainbow of computer pseudocolours, representing low to high calcium concentrations, was motivated by my aesthetic preferences. The compulsion to fill the spectrum of fluorescent proteins from violet to infrared came from the same place.

In 1968, after high school, you joined Harvard University. There, you attended the neurobiology course taught by David Hubel and Torsten Wiesel (who would win the Nobel Prize in Physiology or Medicine in 1981). To what extent did having Hubel and Wiesel (we will meet Torsten Wiesel in Chapter 11) as teachers further shape your research interests?
I was lucky enough to have Hubel as my section leader as well as the head of the entire course. That meant about twelve of us had weekly meetings with him, and he personally graded our assignments. He even invited us to an evening at his home, the only faculty member in my four years at Harvard to treat students so generously. I managed to repair a toy belonging to his son, Eric, so I was pleased to repay his hospitality ever so slightly. I was already interested in the mind–brain connection, but Hubel's course started me seriously towards the study of neurobiology.

In 1979, you started looking for an independent academic position. However, the search was not easy: 'Biological departments considered me a chemist, while chemistry departments rejected me as a biologist.'[11] Do you think that 'labels' and boundaries in science still make sense?
I admit that, personally, I am relatively amorphous and chaotic in my scientific interests. However, most scientists are more conventional in fitting into disciplines, even if newly defined. So 'labels' still have descriptive validity, but they shouldn't become constraining.

Outstanding science doesn't need huge spaces. In 1982, you opened your laboratory in Berkeley. How big was your lab?
The lab was approximately 2000 square feet, or around 180 square metres fairly roomy, but originally without a fume hood, which is essential to do organic synthesis of calcium-measuring dyes. A senior faculty member of my department, Robert Macey, generously donated his fume hood and, more importantly, the ductwork to vent it. It was old, made of wood, and had wire mesh embedded in the glass window. For seven years, all our organic synthesis (including fura-2 and fluo-3) passed through that fume hood, which would never pass safety inspection nowadays.

What were you doing when you received the call from Stockholm? Where you somehow expecting 'that' call?
In California, 'that' call came at 2.20 a.m. I'd taken a sleeping pill so that I could sleep through the night, and the telephone woke me. A few days earlier, Reuters had publicly predicted that I was a possible awardee, along with eight other names in totally unrelated areas of medicine, physics and chemistry. That was enough to get the university publicity office and local newspaper excited and requesting interviews. Monday and Tuesday came with none of Reuter's picks being confirmed, so I felt it was bad luck to be chosen by them. I just wanted the media circus to be over, so I took the sleeping pill. As it turned out, the Nobel Committee was unable to reach my fellow awardees, Shimomura and Chalfie, so when they woke me, they informed me that I alone had to answer the reporters at the international press conference in twenty minutes. So I hope I was coherent despite the sedation.

The lecture you gave in Lindau in 2014 has been one of the most touching and emotional moments of my career so far. I remember you told us of the stroke you'd had and that you felt the urge to write down new experimental ideas in a paper in the *Proceedings of the National Academy of Sciences* (*PNAS*). It had the final lines: 'The present paper has no fresh experimental results but many predictions. Perhaps in a few years, at least one prophecy can be vindicated.'[12] Are you willing to share with us what happened, by giving an account of how you felt, how you went through that difficult period of your life, as well as the joy and satisfaction of putting it behind you?

As I probably described at Lindau in 2014, I assembled my ideas regarding long-term memory in January to February 2013 under the pressure of the deadline for renewal of my neurobiology grant from the National Institutes of Health. Normally, I would never have published these ideas until we had fresh experimental evidence in their favour. But on 26 March 2013, I suffered an intracerebral haemorrhage. While still in inpatient recovery, I somehow developed a gastro-intestinal infection painful and severe enough to make me think it might be fatal.

In retrospect, I was grossly overdramatizing, but I felt that my speculative hypothesis should not die with me. As soon as I had partially recuperated, I converted the grant proposal into the *PNAS* paper, with the assistance of Stephen Adams and Varda Lev-Ram, my most senior co-workers. Why *PNAS*? The most important privilege of election to the National Academy of Sciences is the right to choose referees for a very limited number of submissions to *PNAS*. Subject to regulations intended to prevent conflict of interest, one can choose experts who are also one's friends, which, of course, I did. I couldn't have coped with the nit-picking that's typical of competitive journals nowadays. See the commentary by R. D. Vale in *PNAS* 112 (2015), 13439–13446, which includes humorous speculation on how Watson and Crick would have been rejected too.

---

[12] R. Y. Tsien. Very long-term memories may be stored in the pattern of holes in the perineuronal net. *Proceedings of the National Academy of Sciences USA*, 110 (2013), 12456–12461.

9

Impact Factors

Randy W. Schekman

Not everything that can be counted counts,
and not everything that counts can be counted.

Albert Einstein

Professor Randy Schekman, I will give you three elements: a microscope, a police station and the Nobel Museum in Stockholm. Can you please tell me a life story unifying these elements?
Well, you know the story.

Yes, but I'd like to have the story in this book.
I will repeat the story then. When I was maybe eleven years old, I had a toy microscope as a birthday present. At that time, I was living in California. Near my home, there was a river with some still water. One day I went exploring and looking for frogs. I had a glass jar with me, and collected some dirty water and other things I found on the surface. I came back home and put them on the glass slide. I looked at it and saw a world of all these little creatures – single-celled and multicellular organisms moving. It was fascinating to me. I spent hours in my bedroom looking down the microscope and projecting the light onto a glass screen to explore as much as I could. One evening I recall telling my parents about this at the dinner table. But my father reacted with some scepticism, so I decided to buy a better microscope. I'd saved money that I was earning by mowing lawns and delivering newspapers to buy a professional microscope. But I was never quite able to reach the hundreds of dollars (at that time, around 1961–1962, it was a lot of money) that was needed for the microscope because my mother was borrowing the money and didn't replace it.

I don't recall whether I argued with her or not, but one Saturday morning, when I'd finished the neighbour's lawn, I was upset and rode my bicycle to a police station. I told the duty officer, crying, that my parents were stealing my money and I couldn't buy my microscope. They called my father, and he spoke with the officers in the closed office. My father came out with a rather severe face, but we then went to a shop where there was stuff for resale. And for a hundred dollars, we purchased a student professional microscope, which was wonderful! I used it for many years, until I went to college. I did many annual science projects with my microscope, which was my scientific world. Then I went to college and left it at home. When I finally had a family and bought my own home, my family gave this microscope back to me, but my children weren't very interested in science. So the microscope stayed in the wine cellar in my home. After the Nobel Prize was announced, I got an email message from the Nobel Museum in Stockholm asking me to deliver an object from my past as a reflection of my development as a scientist. It didn't take more than a day to realize that the microscope had a purpose. It's now on display at the Nobel Museum in Stockholm. I went back some years ago, and they told me it's one of the favourite exhibits.

Cool!

When I was there, a group of Swedish students came by: they were standing by the exhibits, and I was asked to give a little speech to them. Life has a strange way of turning out.

Talking about how things turn out, what were you doing when you received the call from Stockholm and what was your first reaction?

I live in California, where there's a nine-hour difference with Stockholm. They made the call at around 10.20 a.m., which was only 1.20 a.m. in California. Of course, I was asleep. I'd just come back from Germany the previous evening, so I was quite tired. But before I went to sleep, I noticed something online that I shared with my wife. It was a report listing some discoveries that had not won the Nobel Prize yet. On the list were the names of Jim Rothman and me, and also Peter Higgs (of the Higgs boson fame). I said to my wife, 'This isn't based on any information. It's just gossip. Let's go to sleep.' But I knew it was the evening the decisions were being made.

When the phone rang, it was 1.20 in the morning. My wife blurted out: 'This is it!' I quickly went to the phone, picked it up and was immediately reassured by a Swedish voice congratulating me and saying it wasn't a hoax. I was shaking at that point. I couldn't think of anything sensible to say, except 'Oh my God!' And then I repeated it to myself. Then I had a brief conversation with the secretary of the Karolinska Institute about what was coming up – we knew each other because we sat on a committee together – and I was able to call some members of my family. First, my father, who every year around early October used to remind me that he wasn't getting any younger and he wouldn't be around forever. He's always had great expectations for me. He was ecstatic. For the next two months, before we went to Stockholm, every time a salesperson called his phone, my father told them, 'I'm not interested in what you're selling, but let me tell you about my son' until the point where the salespeople just stopped calling.

What a story! You won the 2013 Nobel Prize in Physiology or Medicine. You devoted the money from the Nobel Prize to create an endowment for the Esther and Wendy Schekman Chair in Basic Cancer Biology at the University of California, Berkeley. Both your mother and sister, after whom the post is named, died of cancer. What has your relationship been with the concept of disease itself over time both as a human being and as a basic research scientist?
That's an excellent question. My sister died of leukaemia when she was nineteen years old. I was just beginning my senior year in college, and it was a time in my life when I was deeply committed to doing science and research. I was shattered by the experience of her death. My courses suffered and my grades went down, but I knew what I wanted to do, which was science. At that time, I didn't think about a connection between my doing science and any particular use; I came to appreciate this only much later. Basic science, when it works, delivers principles that form the basis of practical applications.

Inspired by my loss, I felt that I had to go on in life. My passion was for science, not for medicine. When I started college, probably because of the influence of my parents, my intention was to eventually go to medical school. In the US, you don't enter the medical curriculum right away; you go to college first and then to medical school. That was my plan initially. But in my first year of college, I realized that the world of science, which I'd explored only as a high-school student, was something that had possible careers and applications. My parents were disappointed, but they eventually got over it. My whole career developed at Berkeley and my discoveries have applications in the biotechnology industry that are very gratifying. I've always enjoyed my working relationships with biotechnology companies. I've served on advisory boards, but I've never felt I was equipped to do work that had direct applications with patients. I was more into discovering the natural world and uncovering how cells work – but always with the conviction that when you make fundamental discoveries, it can help people out practically. And I'm fortunate to see that happening in my own work.

The idea of 'traffic' is notoriously present in our everyday life, whatever it means, from being stuck in a traffic jam to waiting for the bus. You've been studying another type of traffic for most of your life, and you won the Nobel Prize 'for discoveries of machinery regulating vesicle traffic, a major transport system in our cells'.[13] In the future, how will we be able to exploit this transport system to fight diseases?
Our body is made of cells, and different classes of things get secreted from cells. These things are of great importance in modulating the pathways for the traffic of these things themselves. They could be very useful and intriguing in diseases such as diabetes or neurodegenerative diseases. Let me focus just on Alzheimer's disease. The primary genetic forms of Alzheimer's disease are connected through the misprocessing of a membrane protein called amyloid precursor protein, or APP. The enzymes

---

[13] www.nobelprize.org

in the cell that misprocess APP are themselves trafficked by the very same membranes that secrete trafficking proteins. One possible avenue to explore would be to modulate these pathways in tissues where drugs may correct or divert the enzymes that misprocess APP to a different location. APP is made as a membrane protein that travels along the membranes of the cell up to, eventually, the cell surface. Along the way, it covers a sort of intermediate station known as the Golgi apparatus. One of the cell enzymes makes inappropriate cuts in the protein, and when this happens, it generates pieces of APP that tend to aggregate in the brains of patients with Alzheimer's. If you could intervene to divert APP and these enzymes away from each other, you might have a way of blocking the production of this little peptide. Much effort has been expended by the pharmaceutical industry to design chemical inhibitors of the enzyme.

But the trouble with that strategy is that the enzyme is required in development to process other membrane proteins, which are also required for development. So if you have a chemical inhibiting that enzyme, it will have toxic effects. For example, even in adults, it would affect the production of blood cells, because one of the targets of this enzyme is a signalling protein that must be clipped to do its proper function in blood cell development.

The strategy I just suggested would be something else: not to inhibit but to divert the traffic. We need to know a lot more about that traffic pathway to intervene. There are many strategies that could be revealed by learning more basic aspects about trafficking pathways and these molecules. This is just one example. Another is Parkinson's disease. My wife suffered from and died of Parkinson's disease. She was diagnosed over twenty years ago. Her illness progressed into dementia. Some of the genetic forms of Parkinson's disease involve cells that make the neurotransmitter dopamine to remove damaged mitochondria, the little organelles in cells that make the energy currency ATP (and do many other important things).

Cells have an active pathway to cleanse themselves of damaged mitochondria, but there are genetic forms of Parkinson's disease that fail to clear damaged mitochondria. These mitochondria then persist and damage themselves, affecting the viability of dopaminergic neurons; those cells then die, and the patient is deprived of dopamine. If we could figure out a way to intervene in that pathway, which is another membrane trafficking pathway, we might be able to promote the folding control mechanism in these cells to keep them clearing out the damaged mitochondria. Parkinson's disease could be turned into a treatable disease, like diabetes. Once the symptoms become apparent, if you can administer a drug to keep the dopaminergic cells producing dopamine alive, the patient could be sustained for decades with such treatment. Again, intervening in pathways that involve membrane trafficking can have direct applications to disease. But it all requires more basic discoveries about these pathways.

Science is also about competition. How have you dealt with competition at the different stages of your career?
That's also an interesting question. I first experienced that kind of competition when I was a graduate student at Stanford in the laboratory of the Nobel Laureate Arthur Kornberg.

Arthur Kornberg won the Nobel Prize too.
He was the most influential biochemist of his generation, and I learned a great deal from him. The subject I was working on, the mechanisms of chromosome replication, was enormously competitive – we're talking about fifty years ago. We were in direct competition with another laboratory. I used to be nervous when the next issue of our favourite journal, the *Proceedings of the National Academy of Sciences*, arrived because, of course, our competitors weren't telling us what they were doing – sometimes I learned about it only when I read their papers, which was too late. I didn't enjoy that, and, in general, the field of DNA biochemistry and DNA transactions was growing at a great pace. It was just at the outset of

the recombinant DNA revolution. I felt it would be very exciting, but also very competitive in a way that I wouldn't enjoy. When I was finishing my graduate career, I explored areas that I felt I could develop as my own, specifically an area where I wouldn't be dependent on Kornberg's reputation or on my direct experience to do something new. I settled on biological membranes, and through the postdoc, I learned about the work of Jonathan Singer, an influential membrane cell biologist.

In 1974, John Singer wrote a most influential paper on the fluid mosaic structure of biological membranes. I also learned of the work of George Palade, a 1974 Nobel Laureate who elucidated the organelle pathway of protein secretion. In their works, I saw an opportunity for me, with my biochemical experience, to develop a way of finding the molecules that organize the process of secretion.

In 1974, just when I was beginning my postdoctoral work, not a single molecule had been reported with a role in that pathway, which was of enormous complexity. To me, that was an opportunity. I tried to use my own experience and to focus on micro-organisms where that could be studied. I realized that yeast was a perfect test system for several reasons. After all, it's eukaryotic, it has a nucleus, it has an intracellular membrane and it was becoming a very popular organism to study eukaryotic cellular processes – there were well-established genetic techniques that went back to the early part of the 20th century.

That was probably my most important decision. At a very strategic level, by studying the process of secretion in yeast, which no one was doing, I felt I could make a unique contribution. When I was offered a job at Berkeley, I proposed doing that. In the beginning, I was a bit anxious, as I had no experience in that field, had done no genetics and had no preliminary results. My first National Institutes of Health grant proposal on that topic was roundly rejected, but I went on. I had the advantage of a brilliant first-year student, Peter Novick, who was a great addition to the lab. About one year after beginning the experiments, we started having good results. As soon as I saw the first image of a yeast cell with a defect in secretion on the screen of the electron microscope, I knew that what we would be doing for the next twenty years or so was good. It was a very good feeling.

Two days after delivering your Nobel Lecture, you wrote an editorial for the *Guardian* entitled 'How journals like *Nature*, *Cell* and *Science* are damaging science.' When did you decide to write that article? Also, you've published more than forty times in *Science*, *Nature* and *Cell*. Why didn't you write this article while you were an editor at *PNAS* or earlier in your career?

Fair questions. Of course, the path of that *Guardian* piece was a long one, over many years. Yes, I published in those journals as my career was advancing. Some of the same pressures I felt as a young scholar are still felt today: they're prominent venues where people feel the need to publish their work in order to have their work accepted by the broader community to advance their career. But there was a time when I was editor of *PNAS* when I was increasingly feeling that the decisions to publish in journals such as *Cell*, *Nature* and *Science* were being made on the basis of something called the journal's 'impact factor'.

Although the impact factor has existed for decades, it never entered my mind when I was publishing in those journals because it wasn't used prominently in the advertising of the journal. It was a number that we know was created by Eugene Garfield of the US Institute for Science Information to help librarians decide which journals subscribe to. And that makes perfect sense. At some point, this changed into a number that measures scholarship, which it was never intended to be. With increasing distress, journals such as *PNAS*, which had a low impact factor, fell in competition with *Cell*, *Nature* and *Science* because *PNAS* is run by active scientists, people not willing to change the kinds of things they published in order to have a good number. Increasingly, particularly *Cell* and *Nature*, and to a lesser degree *Science*, were unduly influenced by that number in the decisions they made about which papers to consider for review and which papers to publish. I became so irritated by this that I informed the *PNAS* staff and the editorial board that we should avoid using such a number in evaluating the work we published, because it couldn't measure scholarship.

Then, I was given the opportunity of starting a new journal, *eLife*. I felt that it would provide bigger and better chances for me to use that journal to make a statement about how scholarship should be measured. We took a very strong position against the impact factor. I joined forces with other journal editors to promote the 'Declaration on Research Assessment' (DORA), which states quite explicitly that people should move away from the use of that number because it's not a measurement of scholarship. You might ask why I wasn't more vocal or outspoken when I was at *PNAS* or even after I started *eLife*.

Why?

I was as vocal as I could be when I started *eLife*, but, frankly, it's only when you win the Nobel Prize that you have more than a voice. My staff and I and some funding agencies, particularly our colleagues at the Wellcome Trust, thought that Stockholm was a perfect opportunity to make a very strong public statement. It was a group effort to write that editorial. My name is on it, but I can guarantee that there were cleverer people than me who crafted it. It was all very carefully planned to be published on the day of the Nobel Prize ceremony.

We arranged through publicists at the Wellcome Trust to be interviewed live on BBC4, and other editors of the major journals that I was attacking were asked if they were willing to discuss this issue with me. Most of them, wisely, agreed not to. One of them, an editor at *Science*, accepted, although he may have regretted doing so. I'm amazed at how widespread that editorial in the *Guardian* has become. People often talk to me about that, even if they don't know anything about my research.

How do you think the impact of a paper should be assessed beyond any quantitative metrics, or which metrics should we use?

I am dubious that any single number would measure the worth of a paper. I understand that people want to have a surrogate, and maybe there are other measurements. A journal's impact factor is bad for so many reasons. A narrative crafted by scientists to describe their work is the best way to do it.

What I have been arguing when I get this question is the following: we as scientists should adopt a policy of a paragraph describing to an audience what your major discoveries are and how they impact the field you're in. This can be a paragraph of maybe 250 words, and it'll be something that will be part of your CV, a statement that could be read as an initial way to evaluate a candidate for a fellowship or a job.

I use an example of how this works, and it's when people are evaluated for election at the US National Academy of Sciences. For that process, you're nominated by someone. That person assembles a two-page document, which includes a résumé and a list of the twelve most important papers you've published, but I think it's more important that you have to write a 50-word statement and a 250-word statement. One statement is a bullet point for the discoveries for which the person deserves to have special recognition, and the other is an effort to flesh that out for an audience of people who would appreciate the broader and not just the narrow view. As a member of the National Academy, when you're asked to vote for who should be elected, most people are not particularly familiar with the candidates: they read those statements but they don't look at the paper. They make their judgements on whether someone has made an important discovery using the narrative. If we all adopt that, it could be used, and this would be a more accurate reflection of the value of what an individual has accomplished.

In light of this, from a practical point of view, what should change at university and funding agency levels for recruitment, promotion and grant distribution?

Many agencies are thinking deeply about this. In the United Kingdom, the Wellcome Trust is taking a strong and constructive position against the use of the impact factor to evaluate scholarship. In the US, I am most familiar with the Howard Hughes Medical Institute: when an investigator is reviewed for promotion, that person is asked for the five most important papers they've published and, for each of those five, they're asked to write a paragraph to describe their importance.

The people from the panel, those having to judge, read the statements and the papers. And they're told not to look at *where* the papers are published or at the impact factors, but to read the studies, and this is what they do. The National Institutes of Health is doing a similar thing: they've created a biosketch where you have to identify the most important papers and you have to offer a narrative about why they're important. Again, that's an effort to get away from the name of the journals and the impact factor. I feel very strongly about this, and I continue to emphasize this wherever I travel.

In this obsession to publish in *Cell*, *Nature* and *Science*, we have literarily transferred authority for the judgement to professional editors. These are intelligent people, and they're probably knowledgeable, but most of them haven't been in a lab in many years. In my experience, they're not qualified to judge the details of a paper – they rely on scientists to provide critiques – but they hold authority on what goes on in the process and on the final decision. They hold authority on what is published. Part of what we've done at *eLife* is to decentralize this decision by empowering the reviewers and the board members. When papers are reviewed at *eLife*, the reviewers are asked to comment in an online consultation session about the comments made by the other reviewers. The decision is based on an online conversation among the two or three reviewers including the board members, with the aim of coming to a resolution of whether a paper is ready for publication or what else is necessary for the author to complete.

This is an improvement over the standard publication procedure, and I believe the journals who rely on professional editors would not be able to review papers fairly in this way. I am urging my colleagues involved in other journals where scientists are making decisions to use a similar procedure. If we all do that, we might be able to take control away from the largely professional and commercial editor enterprises.

What are the key elements that make a scientific paper an outstanding scientific story to be told?
It has to be based on an original idea, either a new technique or a new way of thinking about a problem, or a brand-new problem that people haven't been thinking about. It's hard to have a formula for that, but the excellent papers are those that, when you read them, you think, 'Why didn't I think of this?' To be brilliant papers, they also have to be written clearly, not embellished too much and not overstated. They should allow the data to speak for themselves. In the greatest papers, the data just stand out.

10

Know Thyself

Venkatraman Ramakrishnan

Know thyself. Nothing to excess. Surety brings ruin.

Delphi Oracle

We don't know what Darwin is doing right now; maybe he's playing backgammon with Isaac Newton, as they rest in Westminster Abbey. Darwin and Newton are two icons of biology and physics. And biology and physics have been two key topics of your life, decades before becoming President of the Royal Society, which lists among its highest honours the Darwin Medal. Aged twenty-three, you did a PhD thesis in physics. At that time, you'd already decided to switch to biology. How difficult was that switch, Professor Venki Ramakrishnan?

It was difficult in one way because I was going 'backwards'. I had a PhD, and I'd just married one year before. I had a six-year-old stepdaughter and a one-month-old son, born about the same time as I submitted my PhD thesis. When I moved to start graduate school all over again, I had two children. My wife had to come with me, and we had to live on the graduate student fellowship. That part was difficult.

Going 'backwards' also meant that I had to take undergraduate courses. I had the idea of becoming a biologist, but I didn't know much about biology, apart from what I knew by reading popular articles in *Scientific American* and other magazines. On the first day of graduate school, they had an introductory seminar where the professors talked about their works, and I didn't understand a thing because of the specific terminology. I didn't even know what lambda was! Lambda, to me, represented a wavelength, whereas for them it was some kind of virus. I had to take undergraduate genetics, biochemistry and cell biology in the first year and slowly build up my knowledge. At the same time, I was doing my graduate research, because, as a 'first-year' researcher, I had to do small research projects before choosing a lab.

I could do this switch in America, which is extremely flexible when it comes to the academic curriculum. You can take whatever courses you need and then do small research projects in the first year to sample what doing research in different areas is like before you settle down. The American system allows you to customize your education.

To get back to your question, that part was difficult, but what made it easier was that I felt I had alternatives. I didn't want to continue the kind of physics I was doing. You shouldn't do anything you're not interested in just because it seems the natural next step. I was interested in fundamental physics and the nature of the universe. When you're young, you have big dreams, but I found myself working on little problems I didn't really care about. By continuing to do physics, I would have continued doing that kind of thing and spent my life doing the sort of boring calculations that no one cares about. I didn't want that kind of life. The only way to escape was to give myself a complete second chance. If something is boring, don't keep doing it. Get out and do something else. Another theme of my life is to keep options open. By switching and starting again, I was keeping my options open.

After attending the graduate programme at the University of California, San Diego and holding a postdoctoral position in Yale, you applied for many faculty positions. However, due to your unusual career choice of a 'physicist turned biologist',[14] you didn't get a single interview. How difficult were those moments? Were you thinking of coming back to physics or even leaving scientific research?

At the time, it was very frustrating. I could have stayed on as a postdoc for another couple of years, but then I'd still have been doing the same work. I'm not sure my CV would have become much better. When you send an application, the person at the other end just sees somebody with a long surname ...

Ramakrishnan.

Who went to a second- or third-tier university for their PhD in theoretical physics, a bachelor degree from India in a

[14] www.nobelprize.org

second- or third-tier place in physics, and applying to a biology or biochemistry department. They probably didn't even know if I could teach properly in English! That was in the 1970s, early 80s.

Moreover, I was using this very 'esoteric' technique to look at ribosomes [cell organelles that synthesize proteins], which required nuclear reactors. This technique had a brief period of popularity, but in biology hadn't really gone anywhere. I didn't have any papers in the 'holy trinity' of scientific journals, namely *Nature*, *Science* or *Cell*. That was the combination of things in my application. If I'd received this application, I would have tossed it in pile B. I don't blame them. It was also about my naivety. I was not very careerist: I just thought that something could be interesting, without considering whether it could land me a job in three years. A lot of people think in terms of career prospects instead of thinking, 'Do I want to do this for a few years?' These people are the careerists: they'll get a job and so on, but I'm not sure they'll end up being very original scientists.

You've always followed your pressing research questions, instead.
Obviously, I made mistakes. Going to a second- or third-tier university is perhaps not such a good idea. I did that twice, for my undergraduate degree and for my PhD. Not because of the faculty: the faculty, even in those places, was pretty good because faculty jobs are hard to get, and you have brilliant people getting them. But they don't attract the best students. You learn from your fellow students as much as you learn from the faculty: the environment is fundamental.

When it was difficult for you to get a position and chase your dreams, did you think, at least once, of leaving everything or coming back to physics?
Never coming back to physics; it just wasn't for me. Don't get me wrong: physics is wonderful, but I think I've 'missed the

boat'. If I'd wanted to be a physicist, I should have made different decisions much earlier. But I'm glad I had that background because it made me appreciate some of the beauties of physics. To get back to the other question, I always had what I called a plan B. I also had a plan C and D, because I was never sure if things would work out, even after getting a leadership position and tenure. Nothing in research is certain. In those days, thanks to my physics background, I was one of the few people who knew how to program a computer. I thought I could maybe get a job at Silicon Valley.

What about the other options?
Another option would have been to retrain as a teacher: high schools are always short of science teachers. If I'd had a teaching certificate and a PhD in physics, I would have been an attractive candidate. I had a family, so I didn't have the luxury of being unemployed. If my A plan didn't work out, I had to have alternative plans. Sometimes I think, 'What if I'd been a computer programmer?' I might have had a great life in Silicon Valley in the 80s: maybe I would have been a billionaire by now. But if I'd become a teacher, I would have had a great profession with the possibility of doing a lot of innovative things. I would have been happy either way. I would have said, 'Well, I've tried science, I gave it my best shot, and it didn't work out. I'm doing something else that is interesting by using my background.'

Your parents were successful scientists. How much did this family background influence your life?
Not directly, but it probably did indirectly. My father didn't want me to go and do basic science. He wanted me to be a doctor. They wanted to make sure their kid was safe and had a good income. I think he wanted to be a doctor but couldn't afford it; his parents were poor and his father died. This was a frustrated dream of his. In the end, my sister went to medical school, and now she's a basic scientist. She was elected as a member of the National Academy. So we all ended up doing

science. My mother encouraged me to do basic science, but I wasn't sure if I wanted to do engineering, medicine or basic science. In the end, I got a prestigious scholarship from the Indian Government. But the condition of the scholarship was that you had to do basic science. I liked physics and mathematics at the time, so that's what I did.

Your mum completed her PhD in eighteen months. How was that possible?
I don't know what her thesis consisted of, but she worked for Donald Hebb, the father of experimental psychology. His ideas are still used by neuroscientists.

Donald Hebb was indeed a pioneer in psychology and neuroscience, and his name is mainly attached to the link between neurons, connections and learning processes.
Part of it was that she'd gone off and left me with my father when I was three years old. I think she felt the family pressure, and that was what made her finish everything quickly. She returned before she was awarded her degree: she submitted her thesis and then immediately came back to India. So I suppose it is possible.

Starting from India, you've worked in many countries.
I also spent two years of my childhood in Australia.

I know. How were your years in Australia?
Sometimes I think of it as some of the most enjoyable times in my childhood. You could run around in the streets in bare feet – a great time.

Was it difficult to come back to India after your Australian stay?
It was difficult but just for a couple of weeks. I do remember I didn't want to come back. I told my father, 'You can leave me with these neighbours!' But, after all, India is my home.

The full motto of the Royal Society comes from the *Epistles* of Horace: 'Nullius addictus iurare in verba magistri, – quo

me cumque rapit tempestas, deferor hospes' ['(being) not obliged to swear allegiance to a master, wherever the storm drags me to, I turn in as a guest']. It looks like the motto of your life. You've been in so many countries: do you still feel yourself an outsider? Where do you feel you belong to?

That's very complicated. When I go to India, it's very familiar to me. When I lived in America – for almost thirty years – I only went to India three times. I strikingly lost touch with India. But then in 2002, about three years after I moved to England, I went to India for my first scientific meeting. Before that, I knew no Indian scientists. That event established my reconnection. If you asked what I feel now, it's complicated: I feel I'm an Anglo-American of Indian origin. There's a little bit of these three countries in me. And if you ask me where my home is, I have to say in Cambridge. That's where I work and I see my friends. But my children live in the US, so that feels familiar too. You just have to think of yourself as an individual rather than as a member of a tribe.

You won the Nobel Prize in Chemistry in 2009 together with Thomas Steitz and Ada Yonath for your work on 'the structure and function of the ribosome'.[14] What were you doing when you received the call from Stockholm?

I remember I came into the lab late that day because I had a flat tyre almost in the middle of my bike ride. It was too late and too far to go back, and I had to walk the bike to the lab. I was a bit annoyed.

Many international prizes on the same research topic I was investigating had already gone to other people, so I thought, 'I'll definitely not get it.' When I got the call, I was almost sure it was a prank. This had become such a joke that there were people in my field campaigning about it – we joked that we'd call some of these people and pretend to be Swedish. But I'd never done it, so I thought somebody else was doing it to me. I had friends at the time who played that kind of joke.

We're halfway through our book. What are the experimental questions that most fascinate you outside your own research field? We will then try to answer some of these in the following chapters.

The big questions in biology are those about the brain and how it's organized. Approaching these questions requires many levels of study, from psychology to the chemistry of memory and circuitry. Lots of new tools will be developed too. The ultimate goal is to understand the self-awareness of consciousness, but I don't know how long it will take. There are other things, such as machine learning and whether machines will ever become intelligent in the way we think of ourselves as intelligent. Then, there are all the aspects of genome modifications and where they're going to lead. Will they, in the end, direct their own evolution? There are a lot of questions in life science.

In physics, there is the discovery of gravitational waves, a 100-year-old theory that has finally been deciphered. Energy physics is becoming so esoteric that it's not easy to understand what's going on. One thing that impressed me was that so much of the universe is dark matter, and so much of the dark energy is beyond understanding. Only a few per cent constitutes our universe and we only see a tiny fraction of the universe as it exists.

I think it's time for a new chapter. Let's start with the brain, then decision making, genetics and the physics of the universe.

11

Memory and Vision

Eric R. Kandel and Torsten N. Wiesel

Problems that appear small
are large problems that are not understood.

Santiago Ramón y Cajal

Professor Eric Kandel, you made groundbreaking discoveries on how memory works, mainly by investigating sea slugs and mice. And Professor Torsten Wiesel, you revolutionized our understanding of 'information processing in the visual system'[15] by studying cats and monkeys as experimental models. Fifty years after your pioneering studies, what do we know and what do we still not know about memory and vision, in a couple of sentences?

Kandel: What my studies showed, for the first time, is that learning and memory involve changes in the structure of the synapses. That principle emerges as a signature in every type of memory we look at. But what is unclear in complex forms of memory in the mammalian brain is what kind of stimulation activates the synaptic systems. This still needs to be worked out.

Wiesel: The point of view that I share with David Hubel, my Nobel Prize co-winner, is that progression in this research field has not been as swift as we had hoped. There have been advancements and discoveries, but we still don't know enough for a solid understanding of the neural basis of visual perception. If you want to understand the brain, you need to have a sense of the neural circuitry and operations. Santiago Ramón y Cajal is undoubtedly a hero for all brain scientists, but there remains a lot of work to be done to bridge the gap between the level of single cells and the operation of cerebral circuits. Perhaps with more advanced techniques, we will be able to further investigate the interactions between circuitry and function.

You mentioned Santiago Ramón y Cajal, the first neuroscientist who, along with Camillo Golgi, won the Nobel Prize 'in recognition of their work on the structure of the nervous system'.[15] More than 100 years ago, Cajal, in his *Advice for a Young Investigator*, wrote, 'There is no doubt that the human mind is fundamentally incapable of solving these formidable problems' such as 'the appearance of consciousness'. In terms of consciousness, cognition and disorder of

---

[15] www.nobelprize.org

consciousness, what is your take on Cajal's quote and how can neuroscience correctly define these concepts?

Wiesel: Considering the techniques and the approaches available during his time, I think Cajal had it right. Moreover, despite many technological improvements, he is, to my mind, still mainly correct. We don't properly understand how cells interact with each other and how a group of neurons can work together. In the future, we should focus not only on synapses, but also on the circuitry that recruits consciousness. I would stick to Cajal for now, but hope that new generations will find ways to understand the secrets of consciousness.

Kandel: Cajal was right, this is a very difficult problem, but we're making progress. For example, the word consciousness can have many meanings. Stan Dehaene, a very good cognitive psychologist working at the Collège de France in Paris, showed, in some beautiful experiments, that if I look at your image, for example, very briefly, just for a few milliseconds, you can see, using certain neuroimaging techniques, that there's a small 'activation' within the visual cortex, but nothing more. Then, if I'm able to look at you for longer, like we're doing now, the activation propagates to a wider region of the cerebral cortex and back again. So the conscious perception involves the spread of information from an initial site to other areas. There is a threshold below which we don't realize that we've 'seen' something, but we have 'perceived it' within the cerebral cortex, which shows a small activation. When we're aware of something, we recruit other brain areas that extend beyond the initial site, and the activation is propagated forward and engages other portions of the brain. But we're still only at the beginning of our understanding of these processes.

Cajal also authored a book entitled *The World as Seen by an Eighty-Year-Old* on memory and vision problems associated with ageing. You were born, respectively, in 1929 and 1924, and we've already met in person a couple of times before today: I can confirm that you're still in good shape. Cajal was wrong on this point …

Kandel: I am visibly in good shape, yes. But when Cajal lived, the average life expectancy for men was fifty or maybe less than that, and women lived a little bit longer. Nowadays, the average age is higher.

Wiesel: [He laughs.] Cajal was speaking for himself! I'm still full of energy, but no longer keep up properly with my former field of research in vision. How old was Cajal when he died?

He was eighty-two years old, already a notably long life for that time. We live and learn and make many decisions. Will a machine be better than us at making decisions?
Wiesel: It depends on what kind of decisions you want the machine to make. There are already machines that are good at making decisions, such as deciding the strategy while playing chess. Automation is coming, and we will no doubt rely on it more and more in the future. Perhaps we may become even more dependent on different kinds of devices. People seem to worry too much that automation will replace the human mind, which is a very remote possibility, at least for now. Tools are often useful. Think about the ATM cash machine: you press a button and get the money. These kinds of automation are beneficial. People are concerned about losing control, but many of us already don't control all of our decisions, so why worry about it? [He laughs.] My father was a psychiatrist and head of the largest mental hospital in Scandinavia. Having grown up in the environment of a psychiatric hospital, I've always been amazed about how people think they can fully control every aspect of their lives.

Kandel: I'm not sure I can answer that. Certain decisions can probably be made better, but for important decisions such as who one should marry or what job one should have, there are too many unconscious and emotional components with which, at the moment, machines can't really help.

A question on the development of neuroimaging techniques to 'look inside' the living human brain. Do you think we'll

ever be able to achieve a live, high-resolution 'movie' of what's happening at the synaptic level inside the living brain?

Wiesel: Right now, I would say no, but the spatial and temporal resolution of some techniques is increasing. If certain techniques can be developed, this would create a very rich field for scientists to study the human mind and brain. I would stick with experiments on animals for now. It's a very ambitious and visionary aim.

Kandel: They're getting better all the time. I'm not sure whether we'll be able to resolve individual synapses in the human brain. Presumably, but it's far away.

There is a topic in neuroscience that has been neglected for a long time and now looks like a game changer in the way we see the central nervous system and its relationship with the whole body: the gut–brain axis. What do we mean when we talk about this?

Kandel: There's a complex nervous system innervating the stomach and the intestine, which is almost autonomous in its own right, but it also communicates with and influences the brain itself. How does it function and how does it influence brain function? This is very interesting.

More broadly, studying the brain has unlimited challenges. It's intellectually very exciting and socially very important. For example, there are many brain disorders we don't have ideal treatments for, such as schizophrenia and mania, to mention just two. We have reasonably good treatments for depression, but, at the moment, we don't treat schizophrenia very effectively. There are many things to do to make life better for those people.

Wiesel: Knowledge about the relationship between the microbiome and the brain is still very limited, but it's important to learn more about the effects on the mind and brain of the gut bacterial flora, and of what (and how much) we eat and drink.

Professor Kandel, do you see Torsten Wiesel every now and then, as you both live in New York?

Kandel: Oh yes, I very much admire him and we get to see each other periodically. We were working together at Rockefeller University when he was President. I also know his wife, Mu, and they're a wonderful couple.

Yes, I know they are. And I've also met you and your wife in Italy, Sweden and in the US, and you're a lovely couple too. I think she's a very important part of your life.

Kandel: She's a very important part of my life indeed. I wouldn't have got the Nobel Prize without her.

Really?

Kandel: She discouraged me from taking any administrative jobs. When I finished my residency training at Harvard, I was offered the Chair of the Department of Psychiatry at the Beth Israel Hospital, part of the Harvard Medical School. I was relatively young and it was a fantastic opportunity. But Denise said, 'What? Swap your research career for an administrative job? Never!'

That's decision making at its finest.

Kandel: Absolutely!

Your wife has the privilege of reading what you write in advance. Is she your best editor?

Kandel: She's a wonderful critic of my work, no matter what I write! [He laughs.]

How did you meet Denise?

Kandel: Somebody told me she was a very interesting woman. I called her up, but she didn't want to go out with me. She didn't want to have anything to do with me. I tried many times until I mentioned the fact that I came from Vienna, and there was a little change in her voice. I think the fact that I came from Europe made her think that I might not be a complete waste of time. Shortly after we started dating, we realized it was serious, and we knew within a few months that we would get married.

Let's move from New York to Vienna. You were born in Vienna and, when you were nine, you went to America with your brother to escape from the Nazis. Before attending New York University Medical School, you studied history and literature at Harvard. How did these studies shape your brain and your mind?
Kandel: Enormously.

In what ways?
Kandel: I got to 'meet' Nietzsche, Dostoevsky and Freud. I'm no longer scared of writing: I learned how to sit down and put something on paper. Since then, I've put together a neuroscience textbook with colleagues and written a couple of smaller books on my own.

'The Kandel', namely *Principles of Neural Science*, of which you are the editor and lead author, is a bible for neuroscientists worldwide.
Kandel: ... and I've authored an autobiography, *In Search of Memory*, and several other books. I'm not scared of writing. This is just one of the things that happen when you major in history and literature. You have a broad education. It was very helpful to me.

Let's imagine you're on the psychoanalyst's couch. [Kandel physically imitates being on a couch.] What has Vienna meant to you?
Kandel: Well, it meant very different things to me. When I was nine years old, they kicked me out of my class and forced me to leave the country. I came to the United States, and I've had a privileged life ever since. I couldn't have found a better place. I had a wonderful experience here. Nowadays, Austria is struggling: it became a democracy, but it has a strong right-wing faction that's quite scary and periodically threatens to take control of the country but hasn't succeeded so far.

How is your relationship with Vienna now, at this stage of your life?
Kandel: Much better than it was before. I've made friends in Vienna, and I help by advising several neuroscience groups there. Vienna is very interesting culturally, and Denise and I have an apartment in Paris and we use our stopovers in Paris to visit Vienna once or twice per year.

When we talk about Vienna, we can't avoid talking about psychoanalysis. What does psychoanalysis represent for you?
Kandel: Psychoanalysis represents for me a fading grey. When I was in college and in medical school, I was in analysis and almost all my friends were too: you couldn't walk down Broadway without bumping into people you knew who were in analysis. Now this is no longer the case. Why? People think that psychoanalysis is expensive, but mainly they think that psychoanalysis has been disappointing. It has failed to do the two things that were absolutely required to survive in a modern world: one, it failed to show that it works better than other forms of therapy; two, it failed to show *how* it works. Outcome studies, or studies with imaging or other techniques, to see the mechanisms by which psychoanalysis works are very much needed.

Why didn't Freud, despite being a neurologist and having a solid anatomical knowledge, ever try to link his psycho-analysis constructs to neuroanatomy?
Kandel: He did. He wrote a paper in 1895 called 'Psychoanalysis for the neurologist': you should look at it. But it's practically incomprehensible. He tried to develop a neurological model that was almost absurd. He said something like: 'We do not know enough about the brain to speak about unconscious and conscious processes. Someday, brain science is going to be mature enough to be able to explain many of the things that I deal with. But, at the moment, we have to develop an abstract cognitive psychological model because we do not have the benefit of brain science.'

Hubel and Wiesel are, along with Kahneman and Tversky – we will meet Daniel Kahneman in the next chapter – and Watson and Crick, one of the most successful collaborations in the history of science. What's your take on the scientific partnership from outside?

Kandel: Hubel and Wiesel was a fabulous collaboration that opened up the study of the cortical visual system. They complemented each other in a very powerful way. They were fabulous.

Professor Wiesel, when and where did you first meet David Hubel, the other half of your uniquely powerful scientific team?

Wiesel: I first met him at a conference in Atlantic City in 1956. At that time, David had already developed and built a device for single-cell recording in the awake cat. I was impressed by the way he approached the scientific problems in the field of cortical neurophysiology and by his sense of humour. At that time, David was at a military research centre, the Walter Reed Army Institute of Research, and I was at the Johns Hopkins Medical School. In 1958, my mentor, Steve Kuffler, invited David and me for lunch together at Johns Hopkins. David was recruited to work in Vernon Mountcastle's group at Hopkins, but his lab was being remodelled. While waiting for the remodelling, Steve Kuffler proposed that David and I start to collaborate in the basement of the Wilmer Institute. At that first lunch meeting, we made plans to record from single cells in the cat visual cortex – and our nearly twenty-year collaboration began.

It was the beginning of a twenty-year collaboration that started in Baltimore and continued in Boston. Your work schedule was rather defined: Tuesdays and Thursdays for recording, Wednesdays and Fridays for analysis, and the rest to analyse the data and plan other experiments. Right?

Wiesel: Correct.

During your first experiments in the basement at Johns Hopkins, you measured the electrical activity of neurons in the visual cortex of the cat while the animal was looking at certain visual stimuli. How long did it take to find the neurons that were responding exactly to the particular visual stimulus you were providing?

Wiesel: Not very long. When David and I started our experiments, we were using an ophthalmoscope specifically built for Steve Kuffler when he did his classical study of recordings from retinal ganglion cells. However, our aim was to record the visual responses from cells in the visual cortex. The first few weeks, we used the same instrument, by inserting a slide producing spots of lights (to be turned on and off) that could be moved on the retina to stimulate cells in the cat's visual cortex. However, we soon found, to our frustration, that cortical cells didn't respond well or at all to these spots.

One day, when we put in the slide, the shadow it produced had the form of an edge. The previously unresponsive cell suddenly produced a burst of spikes. We were puzzled but tried changing the orientation of the edge and moving it across the light-responsive area. After moving the edge of the shadow in many different orientations, we realized that, by chance, the initial orientation was the only one that made the cell give the burst of spikes response. This meant that, by pure chance, we had discovered that a cell in the visual cortex in a cat was selectively responding to a particular line orientation. We immediately recorded from a whole bunch of cortical cells. We found that they all were selective but varied in their orientation preference, falling into more than half a dozen groups of cells with different preferences.

We made this discovery in less than two months and shortly after began to write the paper, which was published in the *Journal of Physiology* in the spring of 1959.

Wow! One of the building blocks of perception! You and David were not enjoying your free time together outside the lab, like going to a restaurant or to the movies with your own families, right?

Wiesel: David and I were spending a lot of time together from early in the morning until late at night or the next morning, and also when we had to process the data, but at the weekend, we usually stayed with our families. I call David my scientific brother rather than my soul brother.

What was the secret behind this successful partnership?

Wiesel: It is hard to pinpoint exactly, but I always say that David was a brilliant guy who could also develop and build our equipment. We enjoyed our collaboration and must have somehow complemented each other.

Did you do something special with David to celebrate winning the Nobel Prize in Physiology or Medicine in 1981?

Wiesel: Not really. When talking about the Nobel Prize before winning it, I always said that 'The longer it takes, the better it is' to avoid interruptions, as there was a lot of work to be done.

I know that after receiving the Nobel call, you went to play a scheduled tennis match with one of your colleagues.

Wiesel: Yes, I had a tennis match at eight in the morning with a colleague, and we played a good game before the press conference.

What kind of tennis player were you?

Wiesel: I've always played with colleagues at about my level of mediocrity. But as a young man, I was interested in various sports and was made Chair of the Athletics Society at school. I've always had the idea of a 'mens sana in corpore sano' [a healthy mind in a healthy body].

Professor Kandel, together with Arvid Carlsson and Paul Greengard, you won the Nobel Prize in Physiology or Medicine in 2000. No tennis for you on the day of the call from Stockholm?

Kandel: No tennis. It was five in the morning. I was sleeping and my wife, Denise, gave me a sharp push and said to me, 'Eric, this is Stockholm calling. It must be for you – it's not for me.'

The history of science is also made up of people who didn't win the Nobel Prize. Who are the people who made the history of neuroscience without winning the Prize?
Kandel: Oh, many people. Vernon Mountcastle, for example, was never acknowledged, despite his major contributions.

In his Nobel Lecture, David Hubel referred to Vernon Mountcastle's discoveries as 'the single most important contribution to the understanding of cerebral cortex since Ramón y Cajal'.[15] Why wasn't Mountcastle awarded the Nobel Prize?
Kandel: I don't know. He made a very important set of contributions. Perhaps his evidence for the columnar organization was not as strong as the evidence that Hubel and Wiesel were able to provide with their own studies. But, despite some weaknesses in his work, Mountcastle was better and more aware than anybody else about the importance of analysing the somatosensory system, and the applications this could have.

Professor Wiesel, both you and Hubel worked closely with Mountcastle at Johns Hopkins at the beginning of your careers. Why do you think Mountcastle didn't win the Nobel Prize?
Wiesel: I don't know. But David and I never worked closely with Vernon, who had his laboratory in a different department.

And when you talked about this with Vernon, what was his opinion?
Wiesel: We have never discussed this. I think he was deeply unsettled over the fact that he didn't receive the Nobel Prize. But the point is not winning the Prize: the important thing is the process of doing science, which, if you're lucky, may open doors to discoveries.

Is it something special for a Swedish scientist to win the Nobel Prize?

Wiesel: It was obviously an incredible experience. When I was a medical student at the Karolinska Institute, I attended the Nobel Lectures. But you have to keep perspective in life.

Professor Kandel, how would you summarize your life in a word?

Kandel: Fortunate!

Really?

Kandel: Fortunate. Very lucky. Look, I came here from Vienna, after being kicked out by the Nazis, and I've had a privileged life. What could be better?

And a huge talent perhaps?

Kandel: I don't know about that. [He smiles.]

12

Words
and People

Daniel Kahneman

POLONIUS:	What do you read, my lord?
HAMLET:	Words, words, words.
POLONIUS:	What is the matter, my lord?
HAMLET:	Between who?
POLONIUS:	I mean, the matter that you read, my lord.
HAMLET:	Slanders, sir.

Hamlet by William Shakespeare

Your fifty years of work had a massive impact on different disciplines ranging from social sciences to psychology, from philosophy to economics. The Prize motivation states that you won the Sveriges Riksbank Prize in Economic Sciences in Memory of Alfred Nobel 2002 'for having integrated insights from psychological research into economic science, especially concerning human judgment and decision-making under uncertainty'.[16] In one sentence, you demonstrated that people don't act rationally. From the very beginning, you were fascinated by the – somehow utopian – possibility of doing psychology with single questions. But how would you summarize who Professor Daniel Kahneman is in a single answer?
I would say that I've been curious about the mind. That would be my answer.

'I will never know if my vocation as a psychologist was a result of my early exposure to interesting gossip, or whether my interest in gossip was an indication of a budding vocation. Like many other Jews, I suppose, I grew up in a world that consisted exclusively of people and words, and most of the words were about people. Nature barely existed, and I never learned to identify flowers or to appreciate animals. But the people my mother liked to talk about with her friends and with my father were fascinating in their complexity. Some people were better than others, but the best were far from perfect and no one was simply bad. Most of her stories were touched by irony, and they all had two sides or more.'[16] Words and people, and words about people, as you wrote in your Nobel biography: have you ever considered a career in psychoanalysis?
Never.

Why not?
It's a completely different discipline, and I wanted to be a scientist. When I was a student, and also now, psychoanalysis

---

[16] www.nobelprize.org

was not considered scientific: that wasn't what I wanted to do. I didn't even want to be a clinical psychologist: I didn't go into psychology to help individuals. I read some Freud, of course, and I spent some time with a famous psychoanalyst, but I was never very taken by it.

You're a leader without a single Twitter follower, an influencer without a LinkedIn Badge certifying it and a very successful writer without a Facebook account. What is your opinion of social networks, and what is your relationship with these 'digital' worlds, indeed made of 'words and people'?
When the social network began, I was too old to be an active participant. I wasn't very keen on it. I think that people of my generation are generally not very active on social media. So there's nothing particularly special in my attitude: I'm a user of email because I was at an age where I could adopt new technologies when email came about, but when Facebook came about, I was too old.

And you don't feel like wanting to learn how to use social media?
No. It's a different kind of interaction with people. There's a sort of 'superficial openness' that you share things with everybody – well, not with everybody but with a lot of people. I haven't grown up that way so it would feel very strange to begin now. I have nothing against it; I'm just not that into it.

Being such an extraordinary scientific mind, what's your take on the post-truth era and fake news?
In a way, this isn't a big surprise. From my perspective, people are not necessarily very interested in the truth. They're interested in things and ideas that make them comfortable. We think we know something when we believe in it, and we can't imagine new alternatives. When knowledge is defined that way, we know many things that aren't true. And indeed, most

of the things we know aren't true. It's not that we believe in things because we have evidence for them – we believe in things because we trust the people who said them. And the fake news is just this brought to an extreme, but it's not a new phenomenon.

Let's keep talking about beliefs. When you were ten, you kept a notebook of essays entitled 'What I write of what I think.' The first essay was on faith, and you were backing Pascal's thoughts: 'Faith is God made perceptible to the heart.' Do you still have that notebook and the same faith?
At some stage in my adulthood, the notebook was lost. When I wrote that essay, it seems I believed in God, but I haven't believed in God for a very long time.

Pascal argues that a rational person should live as though God exists and seek to believe in God. If God does exist, such a person will have only a finite loss – some pleasures, luxury, etc. In contrast, they stand to receive infinite gains – as represented by eternity in Heaven – and avoid infinite losses – an eternity in Hell. What is your take on this now?
My take on this is that you have to believe and put some belief in the idea of total bliss and so on. I don't think that anybody takes Pascal's wager very seriously these days. I don't expect to live after my death.

Your name is attached to the investigation of cognitive biases, namely unconscious errors of reasoning that distort our judgement of the world. Does investigating decision-making processes and cognitive biases help you make fewer mistakes when making decisions?
I don't think so. In a few cases, I've been reminded of things that I know professionally when I was making a decision. In a very few cases, I found this helpful. But mostly I have the same biases I've always had. I'm quite a bit better than I was at detecting other people's mistakes, but not necessarily mine.

Which cognitive illusions are you most often the 'victim' of?
Oh, undoubtedly what I call 'non-regression prediction'. I make
very extreme predictions – I make extreme statements. I'm also
overconfident: I can be very confident in my opinions and then
change them. I'm definitely not bias free.

Did the confidence increase or decrease with age?
I don't think it's changed that much. I was overconfident when
I was young, and I'm probably overconfident today.

You think that everybody should know and be able to name
these cognitive illusions, as they influence our daily behaviour. Is this simple way the best way to make us more aware
of these cognitive illusions and, in turn, to soften their
deceptive impact on our life? Can it be so simple and have
such a huge effect?
I don't believe that knowing about confidence bias has any
direct influence on reducing the effect on our thinking. What
I spoke about in my book was the idea that the way we talk and
gossip about other people can be influenced by the psychology
we know and by the language of psychology.

If there was more psychologically informed gossip, that could
change people's behaviour because we anticipate other people's
gossip. And if we anticipate intelligent gossip, we're going to
act better than if we anticipate unintelligent gossip. I don't
believe that knowing about confidence bias is going to make
you any better.

I guess that writing is, for you, a painful activity with a
rewarding outcome. In 2011, you published a best-selling
book entitled *Thinking, Fast and Slow*. However, you quit
writing it many times, and you were pretty sure nobody
would buy it. That was a wrong prediction. Where was the
overconfidence in that instance?
I'm overconfident in what I believe, but I was overconfident in
believing that the book wouldn't do well. I was completely sure

about that. One can be overconfident and have doubts at the same time: it's not a contradiction. Overconfidence doesn't mean that you believe in yourself necessarily; it means that whatever you believe about the world, you believe maybe more intensely than you should. I always think I can do better when I write, and that I'm not doing the best possible job. I was writing for two audiences: for the general public and for my colleagues. It was very difficult to do both.

What were the reasons not to write it or not to publish the manuscript of the book?
I thought that the book would be disappointing, especially to my colleagues. In that, I was wrong. It turned out that the book has been quite influential within the scientific community, but, at that time, I hadn't anticipated this at all.

The science of happiness is one of the sections of your book and one of your more recent research avenues. How do you think our perception and the measurement of happiness will change in the following decades?
It's very clear that we're approaching a period where data will be collected in an ongoing way: physiological data of various kinds and, quite possibly, brain activity data. When the wealth of data becomes available, I'm sure that the measurement techniques will be broad. We're just at the beginning of this, but one can already see that this is about to happen.

You've been collaborating scientifically with your wife, Anne Treisman, and have written papers with her about visual attention and object perception. Has this been something unique and perhaps special?
No, it was quite difficult. When you disagree professionally within a marriage, it's a little more difficult than when you disagree with a colleague. It was enjoyable but it wasn't simple, because at least on our major paper we didn't really agree. It took us a long time to come to the conclusions.

Your research and your life are associated with Amos Tversky. Kahneman and Tversky is one of the most famous scientific duos alongside Watson and Crick, and Hubel and Wiesel. Amos died six years before you won the Nobel Prize, but he would have been awarded it as well if still alive. How would you describe your partnership with Amos? Can you give us an account of your shared story and tell us the key elements behind it?

The key element was that we enjoyed each other's company. We found each other interesting and funny, so we enjoyed spending a lot of time together. That was one very important element: when you're enjoying yourself, it allows you to be a perfectionist; you never get tired of anything. Work, for us, was a joy, a pleasure. That was one element.

For me, personally – and this is something many scientists know – it takes a long time to understand what your true self thinks: to get it completely clear, to work it out, can take months, sometimes years. For example, my wife had a theory that she published in 1975, and somebody told her that she'd had the idea much earlier. She was very surprised – her main idea for the 1975 theory was in a paper she'd published in 1969, but she didn't realise she'd had that idea. Now, what happened with Amos Tversky and me was that whenever I had an idea, he would understand it immediately. That long delay in working things out more clearly didn't happen. Amos was normally a very critical person, but with me, he was very uncritical. Almost anything I said, he tried to see what was interesting about it. That was very useful and very gratifying. We spent our time improving our ideas. It was all very pleasurable and extremely productive. His interaction with my ideas made them a lot better and clearer: he greatly improved my thinking.

In *Thinking. Fast and Slow*, you wrote: 'The pleasure we found in working together made us exceptionally patient; it is much easier to strive for perfection when you are never bored.' Is it easier to strive for perfection as a duo than as a solo scientist?

Oh yes! When I said 'never bored', it's because we would move continuously between just gossiping or joking or commenting on the day and working: it was one continuous conversation. We both liked talking, and we spent many hours every day just talking to each other. It was much less boring. I don't like writing, and it's an effort for me. With Amos, it was extremely slow, but always interesting and always a pleasure.

Do you think you reached the peak of perfection together?

We clearly did a lot better together than by ourselves, that's very clear.

When writing, an advancement of a sentence or two per day was considered by the two of you as a productive act. The more time passed, the more you got to know each other's minds. Did this reciprocal knowledge gradually turn this slow pace into something quicker and more automated over time, or was it a never-ending bidirectional discovery process between the two of you, as well as with the world you were investigating?

I don't think there was much change in the way we wrote over the years. As long as we were physically together – until 1979 – we did things in the same way. We knew each other's minds very well, but we kept surprising each other.

For many years, you physically spent almost every afternoon together, and one could almost see the two minds merging into a shared idea co-owned by the two of you. Is it true that you tossed a coin to determine the order of authorship of your first paper?

Oh, yes, we did. After that, we alternated the authorship of papers. We did that for a number of years, like ten or eleven years.

Is it a fact or a myth that you statistically quantified that the papers written together received more quotations than your publications as single authors?

There's no question about it: the most frequently cited articles I have are those with Amos, as well as the book I wrote, which I dedicated to him, with the ideas we'd been developing together. Among my top twenty publications, probably fourteen of them are with Amos, and it would be the same for his publications. There's no question. Our work together was the best.

We keep talking about a duo, but what was the role of the so-called 'specter of an ambitious and pedantic graduate student'?[16]

We had a theory in 1975, and for several years we kept looking for flaws and weaknesses in it. We amused ourselves by imagining somebody – a graduate student – who was looking for flaws. Once we found one, we tried to make that person's life difficult. It was a shared joke. Because if, by any chance, the work became important and famous, then people would read it in the normal way, namely with the intent of destroying the work if there were flaws in it. So that's how we did our work, for years, looking at it very critically.

What were the key reasons for the end of your collaboration with Amos?

The key reason was physical separation, which made things much more difficult. Until then, we hadn't really had other collaborators: during the years we were together, we hadn't collaborated with other people at all. But when we were physically separated, it was inevitable that we would develop collaborations with other people: Amos had his students and so on. So that was one part of it. The other part of it, as Michael Lewis wrote in his book [*The Undoing Project*], is that Amos got most of the credit for our joint work, and that created a problem for both of us.

In what sense, specifically?

Obviously, I wasn't happy about it. And I thought Amos should try to fix it. I didn't realize it at that time, but I think both of us knew that the work we'd done together couldn't have been done by either of us alone. It seems almost impossible to tell people: look, it's not just that I collaborated with somebody, but I had to collaborate because I couldn't have done it alone. That's difficult for anyone to say, and it didn't happen. That created some friction. It also created tension because when Amos got most of the credit, it became painful for him to realize that I'd played an essential role in the work. On both sides, this created difficulties.

Michael Lewis's book *The Undoing Project* was about the partnership and friendship between you and Amos. Some of Lewis's books have been made into movies, such as *Moneyball, The Blind Side* and *The Big Short*. I bet one day there'll be a movie about your life and your relationship with Amos. Who would you like to see as Daniel Kahneman on the big screen?
[He laughs.] I have absolutely no idea, and I don't look forward to that. It could very well happen, but I don't know. I also don't know any actors sufficiently well. I can't tell you.

13

Christmas and Carol

Elizabeth H. Blackburn and Hamilton O. Smith

If you know you are on the right track,
if you have this inner knowledge,
then nobody can turn you off . . .
no matter what they say.

Barbara McClintock

Human DNA is packed into forty-six chromosomes inside the cells of our body. At each end of the chromosome are the so-called telomeres: if the chromosome is a shoelace, the telomeres would be the protective plastic ends at the end of the shoelace. Cell divisions are essential to life, and they continuously take place in our body. However, the more the cell divides, the more telomeres are shortened, and the more the cell ages. In return, an enzyme called telomerase 'rebuilds' the telomeres, thus restoring the protection of the chromosome and delaying cellular senescence. The relationship between telomeres and telomerase is a delicate equilibrium. You won the Nobel Prize in 2009 for the discovery of 'how chromosomes are protected by telomeres and the enzyme telomerase'.[17] Unfortunately, sometimes the action of the telomerase is impaired, and telomere maintenance is defective. Which factors negatively affect and which ones favour the action of telomerase, Professor Elizabeth Blackburn?

Chronic stress has been linked to shorter telomeres and reduced telomerase action. But it's not just the stress itself, it's the way a person perceives and deals with that stress that also has a strong impact. A person who finds beneficial ways to cope with stress, such as exercising, getting enough sleep, eating a healthful diet, meditation, positive thinking and social support, will also help protect their telomeres.

In which diseases has an impaired telomere maintenance mechanism been found so far? How are you planning to intervene to restore the regular working of the telomerase for good telomere maintenance?

Impaired telomere maintenance is linked with ageing and ageing-related diseases such as cardiovascular diseases, diabetes and metabolic syndrome, and many cancers. But treating these diseases is not as simple as restoring telomerase. For

---

[17] www.nobelprize.org

example, too much telomerase fuels risks for certain specific cancers, and not only once cancers, in general, have turned malignant. Research has shown that telomerase activity in malignant cancer cells is turned up ten to hundreds of times as high as in normal cells. Finding a way to turn off telomerase, targeting only the cancer cells, might one day be a potent weapon for fighting cancer. Paradoxically, however, some types of cancers are more likely to develop when too little available telomerase makes telomeres shorter. This occurs in blood cancers like leukaemia, in skin cancers besides melanoma, and in some gastrointestinal cancers, such as pancreatic cancer.

Telomerase activity presents a delicate balancing act, and scientists are delving deep into studies about the molecular switches that control this enzyme. Further knowledge may allow us to someday turn up telomerase activity in ageing cells or turn it down in cancer cells. In the meantime, exercise, good sleep, healthful diets and the other lifestyle factors mentioned remain the best bet.

What are the relationships between telomere biology, cancer research and stem cell research?
Cancer cells and developing stem cells both undergo profuse cell division, and that's when telomeres play critical roles. As scientists learn more about the biological mechanisms of telomeres and telomerase, they're finding links to cancer, ageing and stem cell therapies. A deeper understanding of these links may eventually lead to novel interventions for more healthful living.

You and your graduate student Carol Greider, Nobel cowinner, discovered telomerase on Christmas Day in 1984. Do you still remember the excitement of that day? What was it like?
I do remember it. We'd been working for six or seven months on this project with no proof that we were even on the right path. Then Carol came into the lab and found this wonderful

Christmas present. The next day, there we both were, looking at this gel, or autoradiogram, that showed distinct bands regularly spaced apart. I remember thinking they looked like the markings on a tiger's tail. I had this feeling in my gut that we'd done it: we'd found evidence of a new enzyme, telomerase.

When Carol and I looked at each other, I knew we were both thinking the same thing: this was a big discovery, a really big discovery. But, of course, if you're a good scientist, you call up your scepticism and start developing hypotheses about why it couldn't possibly be what you think it is. I'd say it took another six months of experiments before we allowed ourselves to believe our discovery.

Your husband, John Sedat, is a scientist and has been collaborating with you. In your Nobel biography, I read that for love, after getting married, in 1975 you switched your postdoctoral fellowship from the University of California, San Francisco to Yale, where your husband had a position, and the two of you went to California three years later. For many couples in research, it's not always easy to find two positions in the same university or at a short distance. Are you aware of any university worldwide having a scheme for couples in research? What should be done to help families where both partners are in science?
A good number of universities in America are already supporting dual-career hiring in their written policies. It's a sound investment. I believe somewhere between thirty-five and forty per cent of faculty members in this country are married to other academics, so keeping them at the same university or institute only enriches the overall faculty. Rather than the commonly used term 'two-body problem', I like to think it is a 'two-body bonus'.

In line with this, do you think universities and societies are supportive enough when it comes to helping researchers with children?

It's not just universities and research institutes that need to address the issue of balancing career and childcare, it's American society in general. The United States trails many European countries in how it values, supports and accommodates childcare.

Scientific research is a field known to require long and irregular hours. Researchers are often ruled by the experiments they're running and must be in the lab late into the night and on weekends. The demands of the work are compounded if both parents are scientists. Wouldn't they be able to focus on their work better if they knew that their children were close by and well supervised? If science is a field that looks into the future, perhaps it's the one that needs to initiate this change in attitude and priorities.

Let's talk about other key issues in academia, education and research. What is your view about the continuous increase in the cost of education? What will be the consequences?
I suspect there are many bright and talented people in countries all around the world who don't have the economic resources to obtain the sort of advanced education that they need and deserve – and who might never be able to deliver their talents to society. That's a loss to everyone. Education can't become a privilege of the wealthy. Society must institute changes to make quality education available to all who desire it.

Will online courses one day replace in-person courses? How significant and how negative can the lack of direct contact with teachers and potential mentors be?
I don't believe that online courses will ever supplant focused instruction and thoughtful discussion between a professor and his or her students. While online courses can dispense information much the same way that textbooks can, true learning develops through inquisitive and challenging discourse. It is sparked by a colleague's observation or a pointed remark by a

professor. Science requires a community of minds and lively discussion to provoke the most innovative thinking. Plus, let's not forget the importance of the one-on-one relationship between a mentor and a student. A good mentor shares the broad perspective of experience and constructs personalized guidance to help a student fine-tune their thinking and add focus to their research. A good mentor also provides just the right sort of encouragement and praise to build confidence. That's something that online courses can't provide. Yet online courses for those with no alternatives are an important step, otherwise many educational possibilities would be out of reach.

You were supervised by a Nobel Laureate, Fred Sanger, and you supervised a Nobel Laureate, the aforementioned Carol Greider, a somehow unique combination. Data show that only around one PhD student out of three gets a postdoctoral position, and only a tiny percentage manage to get a permanent academic position.[18] How should we cope with this? Some ideas: should perhaps access to the PhD study be restricted, should more tenure-track positions open or a scheme for researchers not staying in academia be created, for example by fostering the link between academia and industry?
Having guided the training of hundreds of young scientists over the years, I care deeply about their career prospects. They are the future of science. The good news is that employment opportunities are expanding as more organizations collaborate to advance biological research. Some of these opportunities are in academia, while others arise in equally important facilitative areas, such as lab management, business development, science policy and communications. For some PhD students, those options might lead to very satisfying careers. Here in

---

[18] The Royal Society (2010). The Scientific Century: Securing Our Future Prosperity. https://royalsociety.org/~/media/royal_society_content/policy/publications/2010/4294970126.pdf

America, the National Institutes of Health has initiated a program called BEST, Broadening Experiences in Scientific Training, to offer graduate and postdoctoral students exposure to non-academic careers in science. Rigorously examining your passion for science and then educating yourself about your options will guide you to the right choice.

In light of these considerations, are there some aspects of the PhD experience that you would change or shape in a different way to make the PhD even more 'spendable' in the job market? Scientists are critical thinkers. We're good at examining the facts and making decisions based on facts. As the environment of biological research is changing both inside and outside the lab, I encourage PhD students to stay apprised of these changes. Know your options. Get involved. A group called Future of Research, for example, which began as a network of postdoctoral volunteers, became a fully-fledged non-profit organization. They're working to educate aspiring scientists and to effect change in science policy. It's a good start.

In 2002, you were appointed as a member of the President's Council on Bioethics. As you recollected in your Nobel biography,[17] you have publicly made clear that some of your opinions were not in line with the Council's recommendations or with the views of the White House. In 2004, the Personnel Office of the George W. Bush White House informed you that you would no longer be part of the Council. What did the dismissal from the Council represent for you? What were the consequences of that act on your way of thinking and behaving?
The service on this Council and the dismissal did nothing to change my way of thinking or behaving. As a scientist, I stood up for sound scientific fact, and I still do. I was rather surprised that the incident garnered so much attention worldwide, and I was pleased by the support I received from a much wider community than just scientists. I suppose the impact of my stance hit home when a colleague of mine, who was receiving

a prestigious award at a ceremony, turned to me and asked, 'What does it feel like to be a symbol?' I guess I'd have to say that it felt rather good.

What have you learned from that experience?
That to have a healthy science policy that best serves society, we must maintain an environment of openness to available scientific evidence and encourage the exchange of ideas. We don't know where all of our advances in understanding biology are headed. But to realize the full promise of research, we mustn't fear new science. As one of my heroes, Marie Curie, said, 'Nothing in life is to be feared. It is only to be understood.'

You won the Nobel Prize in 2009, the same year that saw Barack Obama win the Nobel Peace Prize. Have you exchanged thoughts with him about that experience?
No, not my own thoughts. However, I did have the opportunity to congratulate him personally shortly after the news. I went to the White House to meet him, because it has become customary for US Nobel Laureates to meet the President the year they're awarded the Prize.

More generally, are you still in touch with the people who won the Nobel Prize in 2009? Do you have some great shared memories with them of that Nobel Week or of how each of you spent that week as a fulfilling experience at a personal level?
I'm not in regular contact with the other 2009 Nobel Laureates, except for my co-winners and colleagues, Carol Greider and Jack Szostak. Sometimes I cross paths with the others at international conferences and we talk. One of my favourite memories of that week is sitting inside the beautiful Royal Bernadotte Library in Stockholm for a round table discussion of our research, our early lives, our inspirations and ambitions. It was interesting to discover that many of us had had similar childhoods: we each had a hunger for knowledge at an early age and seemed to have known what course of study we wanted to pursue.

Let's have a look at some data, and Professor Hamilton Smith is joining us. The disproportion between the number of male and female Laureates is massive: the ratio of males to females is about 17:1. What are your thoughts on these numbers?

Blackburn: Humanity is being short-changed. Advancements in philosophy and literature and medicine and science require a diverse array of minds, and that includes both men and women.

Smith: Historically, the incentives and opportunities for women to pursue higher education and research careers were restricted culturally. Marie Curie was an exception. While some cultural influences still exist, times have changed. I believe that men and women are equally endowed so that things will even out in the future.

2009 still represents the record for the most Nobel Prizes awarded to women in a single year [five]. Do you feel that things are changing or was 2009 an exception?

Blackburn: I'm optimistic. I do believe things are changing, although perhaps too slowly. There are many extraordinarily talented women in this world, and they're finally being recognized for pioneering the sort of thoughtful research that impacts humanity for the good.

Smith: Things are changing, but 2009 was an exception without a doubt.

In your Nobel biography, you remarked that Nobel Laureate Barbara McClintock advised you to trust your intuition more often on scientific results. How much space is left for intuition in contemporary science?

Blackburn: I'm picky about that word 'intuition' because it implies knowing something is going to happen or sensing the path one should follow. I prefer the word 'curiosity,' *not* knowing what is going to happen and being open to travelling an unexpected path. I believe that science is as creative an endeavour as the humanities. Doing good science is letting the imagination be open to new ideas and lateral leaps that might at first seem outlandish. I call that curiosity-driven science.

Smith: Intuition is essentially guessing based on knowledge. There is always room for it, but most achieve their discoveries and inventions by hard, steady work.

Rocket Science

Kary B. Mullis

Just take your time – wave comes.
Let the other guys go, catch another one.

Duke Kahanamoku

Professor Kary Mullis, the discovery of PCR, short for polymerase chain reaction, allowed us to 'photocopy' the DNA, and you're the man behind the discovery. Kids usually take sugar from their mum's kitchen to eat it, whereas you often used it in a mixture with potassium nitrate to fuel homemade rockets.

We had access to a nice, tiny grocery store where we could buy candies.

Once, you blasted a frog into the air (and got the frog back alive).

Yes. I could also calculate with a stick the angle and the distance from the ground: it was a mile high. Although I had to spend a lot of time improving the design of the rocket, that was a good way of spending the summers.

That's rocket science! Wasn't your mum a bit concerned about your first approaches to science?

I can remember her at the window, watching my friends and me. Once we burned a tree. She was rather permissive, but not neglectful. She watched us, but she didn't know what we were doing or understand what was happening. She didn't understand what it was all about, but she understood there was fire involved and potential dangers. I knew what happens when you mix sugar and potassium nitrate: you can fuel a rocket. She advised me not to blow my eyes out. I replied, 'OK, mum, I'm not going to hurt myself.'

How important has your mum been throughout your life?

I was closer to my mum than my dad. My dad travelled a lot during the week. All my friends liked my mum, and she liked having my friends around our house. She was a nice lady. The house where we lived was pretty large. A nice thing my mother did was to give us a kind of private space. She was mainly at home until I was well into high school. At a certain point, she started a business.

Is it true that she used to send you articles about DNA from the *Reader's Digest*?

For a long time, she didn't understand that I didn't need these articles. And that was a kind of funny thing.

I reckon you learned a lot about organic chemistry by having free access to the chemistry lab during high-school years.
Yes, I first started doing organic chemistry experiments in high school. I had a teacher who gave us permission to use the chemistry laboratory in the afternoons. We hung out there, and our teacher liked the fact we enjoyed that. During the summer, I also had a job in a business, and Max, whom I worked with, quickly recognized my talent and that I could understand the structures and names of the chemicals. We became friends. With some other friends of mine, we started making chemicals that weren't commercially available, which was a fun summer job. One of our first jobs was in a house garage. We had a sign on the door saying: 'Do not come in.' But their grandmother came in, and we had to move to a different location. Then I went to graduate school, and I left for California.

The first laboratory you joined was a biochemistry laboratory (with very few rules).
Yes, at Berkeley. I didn't really bother with molecular biology courses. Molecular biology was just starting to grow and it wasn't as biological as I'd thought it would be.

At that time, you already knew a great deal 'hands-on'.
And I was a quick learner. Chemistry was in my mind all the time when I was making chemicals and stuff. It was a good way to learn.

Therefore, you decided to enrol on an astrophysics course instead of molecular biology. You published your first scientific paper in *Nature* in 1968!
Yes, the title was: 'Cosmological significance of time reversal.' It got accepted almost straightaway.

Why did you choose a different career path over astrophysics?

I thought that astrophysics was very interesting, but you can make a living as a biochemist. An astrophysicist seemed more of an academic kind of thing. And, in a way, you don't really do experiments in astrophysics.

The PhD committee that approved your doctoral studies in molecular biology (without taking molecular biology) was composed, among others, of the Nobel Laureate in Physics Donald Glaser, one of the founders of the biotech Cetus Corporation, where you would later work, and Daniel Koshland, the editor of *Science*. He first rejected your PCR paper, your Nobel discovery.
Yes, he didn't see that the PCR thing was a big deal; he missed that. There were some letters back and forth between Koshland and me, with me saying, 'You have to publish it – this is a big deal' and Koshland replying, 'We have other things to publish.' I think it's the biggest mistake Koshland ever made.

At that time, when you were defending your PhD thesis, did you ever imagine how important these people would be to you in the coming years?
I wanted somebody on the committee who could appreciate astrophysics, although it wasn't easy to find someone in a department of biochemistry and molecular biology who was also an expert in physics. At least Glaser knew what the concepts were in physics and understood that I had published a paper in *Nature* about astrophysics.

As you recall in your biography, your 'eureka moment' happened in 1983 while driving your car in Mendocino County, USA, 'at mile-marker 46.58 on Highway 128'. Ten years later, on your mum's birthday, you received the call from Stockholm. What did you do immediately after that?
I went surfing! At that point, it was my custom to go surfing every morning with Steve, a friend of mine. Steve came over to my house right after I got the phone call. The guys from Stockholm said, 'Don't be surprised if your phone rings all day long.' Then we went surfing.

You went surfing, and then you pretended someone else was Kary Mullis to throw off the press!

When we came out of the water from one of my favourite surfing places, the press had figured out where I was – I think they'd asked other people who lived around me where I used to go surfing in the morning. It was a fun day.

I imagine it was.

At that time, I understood that the Nobel discovery would make a big difference for biochemistry. I didn't think about how fast the technique would spread. I knew it had the potential to spread because it was easy to do. The world was set up and ready for this discovery. It was certainly necessary. It seems that somebody else could have done it, but nobody did. I remember someone I met afterwards who said to me that nobody was behind me in the race.

PCR is one of the most important discoveries of all time. It changed the world in many ways.

It's all over the place. Every issue of *Nature* has a paper using it. Now it's just normal to use it.

In 1983 you made your Nobel Discovery, and in 1993 you went to Stockholm. In 1998, you published your autobiography entitled *Dancing Naked in the Mind Field*. If you could add new chapters, what would they be about?

I'm not sure right now what they'd be about. There are a lot of exciting things on the planet now, especially in science.

Do you regret having done or not having done something during your life?

Any particular things I've not done yet? No, I don't think so. The idea of writing a new book does appeal to me. But the one thing that is clear about life, in my case, is that I haven't maintained the same sharpness or quickness of brain that I used to have.

What is your advice for future generations of scientists?

I don't know how to answer that question. Right now, if I were twenty years old and just starting graduate school, what would

I be drawn to? Before PCR, one of the things I was interested in was becoming a computer scientist. I was writing programs and understood that computer science was an interesting way of not doing the same thing over and over. The computer offered the possibility of writing a small program, and every time you have to do that task, you can just run the program.

Concerning the advice, I would say do something you enjoy and be willing to change track if you don't. When you go to scientific meetings and they have poster sessions, spend time with the people standing by the poster and figure out what it's about. There's always someone there who will be happy to explain what it's about. I enjoyed meetings with poster sessions because you had the chance to speak to somebody who knows everything about a specific topic.

I didn't recognize boundaries. There was nothing too weird that I wasn't interested in. There was nothing too complicated if I wanted to know more about it. I combined many things to come up with PCR. Having no boundaries meant that sometimes I was also a little bit weird socially: it's part of who you are. A small example: while walking along the street with my love, Nancy, if we see some amazing flowers outside a building, we'll go and have a chat with the owner about them. We also like collecting seeds from different parts of the world for our garden, and I like planting small trees.

I know you love surfing (well, many people know this: a picture of you surfing is on the cover of your book, *Dancing Naked in the Mind Field*). What did surfing teach you?
Just to have a lot of fun! You're not always aware of why certain things make you who you are. And surfing was a very social thing: while waiting for a wave, we usually talked to each other.

You started your Nobel Lecture by quoting two of your scientific heroes, the Nobel Laureates Max Delbrück and Richard Feynman, and the book *What is Life?* by Erwin Schrödinger. In a couple of sentences, what is life?

It's still a pretty good question and a relevant one, even after all these years. Life turned out to be more mystic than I used to imagine. I've had experiences that were just totally weird, and this affected my vision of it. Once, I had contact with my just-dead grandfather in my house: I talked to him for at least an hour, maybe two. I hadn't known he was dying, and when I called my brother the next morning, saying that I'd talked to him at my house, my brother told me that he'd died the day before. I was in California, and my grandfather had died on the East Coast. He came by my house to see me on his way out – that's the way I looked at that experience. Experiences like this change the scepticism you might have in saying that life is just a chemical process and has nothing to do with the spirit. Life is more complicated than biochemists understand. To the question 'What is life?' there's no more answer today than there was decades ago. It's been asked so many times, and I don't think anybody, including Erwin Schrödinger, has any idea of what it is.

15

The Big Bang
Practice

**Arno Allan Penzias, Hamilton O. Smith
and David J. Gross**

We especially need imagination in science.
It is not all mathematics, nor all logic,
but it is somewhat beauty and poetry.

Maria Mitchell

Professor Arno Penzias, you discovered, with Robert Wilson, the 'cosmic microwave background radiation',[19] which helped establish the Big Bang theory of cosmology. For this, you won the Nobel Prize in Physics in 1978. Briefly, you were using an antenna to capture signals. A strange background noise remained after all the interferences had been eliminated. After checking the equipment, removing pigeons nesting in the antenna and cleaning out their droppings, the noise remained: the cosmic microwave background radiation.

It is always said that outstanding scientific achievements appear when luck meets preparation. One can't do without either of them. In my case, a number of things happened in sequence. When I started doing radio astronomy, I wanted to know something about the world we live in. My idea was that we're in the Milky Way, but there are other objects that aren't. The first thing Bob Wilson and I did, using our instrument, was to try to measure objects that were clearly extragalactic. Once we were able to discover stars in other nearby galaxies, we made a list. We did a series of experiments that allowed us to understand clearly which of these objects were extragalactic and which weren't. This wasn't original work, because many people had done this early on when recognizing extragalactic objects. But in our careful work, after having done all this, we noticed additional background radiation. The more we kept doing this, the more we found that there was background radiation. We thought it was leftover radiation that was not associated with any other object.

You're the author of two books: *Ideas and Information* (1989) and *Harmony* (1995). In these books, you define many key concepts and relate them to the past and the future. Specifically, in the Preface of the first one, you wrote: 'I have no doubt that the world's most powerful information

---

[19] www.nobelprize.org

tool will continue to be the human mind.' Are you still of the same opinion?

I think so. The human mind is something that somehow, from evolution or the Creator, allows us to think. Either way, it's an amazing gift that allows us to be curious creatures.

Lindau is always a gathering of great minds.

I would like to say that my Lindau experience is clearly something that lifted my spirit; it was a huge benefit to me. It allowed me to unify my pre-work and post-work experience. I remember in Lindau thinking that we had unbelievably brilliant students. To me, the greatest satisfaction I've ever had was the joy and energy of bringing these students physically together with the older scientists from whom they were learning. A fantastic and wonderful experience. The nice thing about Lindau is also that there's no end to it – at least we hope not. It's like the water cycle from the ocean going into the sky and becoming snow, and the snow falls back to the Earth and goes into the lake. As living creatures and human beings, we are allowed to enjoy it and grow with it – and contribute to it.

When talking about Lindau, we can't avoid talking about your advice to young scientists.

I would say you have to be prepared to be wrong, because otherwise you'll stay on the same path, but this path won't lead you where you need to go. Also, be prepared to accept contradictions.

Now let's start with a series of dichotomies. Professor Hamilton Smith, whom we have already met in previous chapters, will join us for some questions. Competition versus collaboration in science – which is best for the progress of science and why?

Penzias: That's a very good question. I'd like to say both, but if I had to say one or the other, competition. When you're competing, it's crucially important to compete with an open mind.

Smith: I have a few scientific friends who've been spurred on by competition; however, I much prefer collaboration. There's no greater pleasure than working on a problem with colleagues whose ideas are both synergistic and complementary to your own. A perfect example is Watson and Crick. Watson's book *The Double Helix* details how the two of them interacted and kept each other going to overcome one roadblock after another – Crick with a physical approach versus Watson with a biological approach. Crick deduced that DNA must be a helix and Watson figured out the base pairing and its implications. Some have pointed out the imagined competition with Linus Pauling and it makes for a good movie script, but that's not what motivated them.

Early in my career, I was lucky to have a graduate student, Kent Wilcox, ask the right question. He observed that foreign DNA was destroyed after being taken up by the bacterium *Haemophilus influenzae* and asked whether it might be a restriction enzyme. Unfortunately, he was drafted a couple of months later. But before he left, we decided to look. I then worked alone for several months. Fortunately, at the end of the year, I was joined by a brilliant postdoc, Tom Kelly. Working together during a time that was undoubtedly the greatest of our lives, we were able to solve the sequence of the cutting site in a few months. Alone, it might have taken much longer.

Professor David Gross, Nobel Prize winner in Physics in 2004, will join us for a couple of questions. Ideas versus technology – which one is more important to lead to future breakthroughs?
Penzias: I would probably say ideas because I think that technology will take care of the job somehow. Technology tends to overwhelm us anyway. We use technology to sort ideas out.

Smith: Both are equally important. Let me elaborate. New technology opens up whole new vistas of research. Take, for example, CRISPR technology, or the bubble chamber in physics, or restriction enzymes, or DNA sequencing. On the other hand, new ideas such as relativity, Maxwell's equations and the periodic table have had a profound influence on spurring new technology and new ideas.

Gross: I don't like the way you put it. Technology or application of knowledge to create new tools, new products and new methods or objects requires lots of new ideas. Perhaps we can talk about basic science versus applied science. Or acceleration of nature and development of new knowledge, new understanding. They go hand in hand, in both directions. If you want new technology, you have to have new ideas. But it's also important to have great basic science to drive innovations and tools to explore the ideas. Biology nowadays is driven by new tools, many of which come from physics, to measure biological processes. Technology is essential for progress in science, which is essential for advancement in technology.

Where do great ideas come from?
Penzias: They come from the human mind! Fortunately, nature has created us as very curious people.

Smith: That's a hard one. Isaac Newton is quoted as saying that he could see further than most because he stood on the shoulders of giants. It's my opinion that almost all new ideas have been hinted at in past work. Very few ideas are truly 'eureka' events.

Gross: Good question. My feeling is that we understand very little about the human brain and how it works. I'm sure you have the same experience – even when I'm talking to you, the answer comes from somewhere. Based on my experience, my feeling is that a lot of what becomes conscious in my brain, which I can either say or write, is in some place in the brain that is working away and of which I'm not conscious. I don't even understand where my ideas come from! We know so little about what goes on inside the head. There are, however, ways we've learned to stimulate new ideas: we practise those over and over again. But I don't think that anyone knows the answer to this question.

In your books, Professor Penzias, you didn't mention God very often despite, I guess, playing an important part in your life. I checked in the index, but there is no God there (He should have been between Global Economy and Gore, Al). Are you keen on defining God?
When I go through all that I've done and all that has happened in my life, I came down to the last possibility, which is that I hope there is a God. I deeply hope there is a God.

Is there more faith in science or in religion? Which one is more dogmatic?
Penzias: It's hard for me to separate science and religion. We always do things as either one or the other, in a very narrow sense. But if we include both of them, what we're talking about is the human mind versus the human spirit. It's hard for me to see them as separate things. It ultimately comes back to a system where it's a mixture. At different times of our life and under different circumstances, we switch from one to the other. Also, instinct and logic go together: I don't have any means to separate them.

Smith: You're asking the wrong person. I have no interest in or understanding of religion. My father and mother were Southern Baptists by upbringing, but one day when I was around seven, I asked my mother why we no longer went to Church. She said that one Sunday (when I was about four), she and my father awoke, started getting ready for Church and then suddenly looked at each other and said, 'Why are we doing this?' So, I was brought up with no religious indoctrination. Science, to my way of thinking, is not a faith. It's an attempt to understand how the world works, how our bodies work and why we exist. There's also a desire to improve our lives through technology.

Gross: We often say we believe in various things in science, by which I mean something very different from religious beliefs.

Science has ways of judging the truth of statements and beliefs, theories and models, using scientific understanding. We have scientific methods to define what is true or not. We continually subject these beliefs to experimental tests and observations. We endeavour to make predictions about things we've observed based on these ideas, beliefs and theories, and we confront these predictions with nature. This is the scientific method, which is very different from the belief of religion, where the authority is unquestioned. There's no comparison: it's totally different. However, I admit that it's not applicable to all the questions we might ask. Religion is open to any questions, such as the meaning of life, a question I'm often asked when I give a talk about the scope of physics. I say there are questions science can't answer, but that religion and philosophy sometimes try to answer. Part of the scientific approach is the limit of questions that we hope to answer.

16

Houston, We Have a Solution and Many Questions

John C. Mather

ANDREA: Mother says we must pay the milkman. If we don't, he'll soon be making a circle round our house, Signor Galilei.

GALILEO: The expression is: he will be describing a circle, Andrea.

ANDREA: All right. If we don't pay, he'll be describing a circle round us, Signor Galilei.

Life of Galileo by Bertolt Brecht

Professor John Mather, you've been a key player at NASA for a long time, winning the Nobel Prize in Physics in 2006 and being one of the 100 most influential people in the world according to *Time* magazine's list in 2007.
Yeah, that's a bit optimistic, but this is what they say.

And you were also 'a big fish in a little pond' who didn't know 'what was yet to come in the big world',[20] as your parents reminded you frequently in the 1960s.
Yes.

Let's start with a cliché: where was the twenty-two-year-old 'big fish' when man landed on the moon? What is your memory of that event?
I was a summer camp counselor, putting nine-year-old boys to bed. We were at a small camp in the Finger Lakes of New York state. There was only one small television, and I wasn't watching it because I was busy. I didn't know how important it was going to turn out to be. At that time, I was really excited about fundamental physics, and I didn't know how important NASA was going to be for science.

I know that when you were a kid, your parents enjoyed reading aloud from various books, including a biography of Galileo. To sleep and to dream, I guess?
Yes!

There's a sentence in Brecht's Galileo that says: 'Unhappy the land that is in need of heroes.' But a young adolescent needs heroes. Who were and are your heroes in your personal 'hall of fame'?
It started with Galileo and Darwin. Then I got to know what Einstein had accomplished, and when I finally learned what he'd done in 1905, I thought it was astonishing. There's no way any of us can keep up with him: the story goes that he had three or four Nobel Prize-winning discoveries all in one year.

[20] www.nobelprize.org

And I'm still a little bit stunned to see my name on the same Nobel list in Stockholm. Richard Feynman was a hero for me: when I was a graduate student, I wanted to be like him, so I chose to be a theoretical physicist. I thought it was exciting, but then I met people who were already better than I was. And at that time, in the early 70s, someone told me that there weren't enough jobs for theoretical physicists. He asked: 'Are you wealthy?' I replied, 'No, I'm not, so I don't think I'm going to do that.'

In the same period, I was spending my days at the library writing, but I wanted to be part of a laboratory. It was much more sociable doing things with other scientists than being in a library. I enjoyed making that transition, even though I'm not that great at building things. Among other heroes, I would mention my thesis adviser, Paul Richards, who sent me in the direction I am now. There was also my postdoctoral adviser, Pat Thaddeus, and Mike Hauser, who was not only my boss for many years but also the best man at my wedding.

What was your feeling when you were designing your first mission?
The first feeling was that although we were trying to design our own project, we might not be chosen. We didn't know how many competitors we would have. It turned out that there were 150 responses to the 'call for proposals' from NASA. I realized that our chances were surely minimal and we didn't have to worry about winning. Later, when it seemed that we might be chosen to do something, things started to become serious. I was a postdoc in a small NASA laboratory in New York, the Goddard Institute for Space Studies, and then I was recruited to a bigger NASA lab in Maryland, where I still am. When I came here, it became evident that we might actually be able to realize our project: the ideas were good, and we were assigned to work with professional engineers and management teams. The intensity increased, and it's been a high-intensity job ever since!

Your name is linked to COBE, which stands for Cosmic Background Explorer, a satellite to study the cosmic microwave background radiation. It was initially planned for 1988, but the Challenger explosion delayed that plan. What did that huge tragedy mean for an insider at NASA and how did it impact your work pipeline?

I was working on the COBE satellite at the time we heard about the Challenger explosion. I thought that it was – and is – a tragedy, but it was not totally unexpected. Those flights were much scarier and riskier than the public knew. But we didn't appreciate how dangerous it was until the tragedy happened. My immediate question was, 'What are we going to do now?' My job was to continue working on the COBE satellite project, although I didn't know how this was going to happen. Pretty soon, it became clear that the project management had ideas on how to keep the project going.

COBE was supposed to be launched on a space shuttle, and we didn't know how this would happen. My manager found a way to replace it with a 'Delta rocket'. It was also decided to remove half of the material originally planned. We found a way to re-engineer it. Only a few things had to be changed in the instrument package, but the spacecraft portion had to be completely rebuilt. Paradoxically, these changes were extremely lucky for us. We got permission to use a Delta rocket, which seemed like a wonderful miracle. At that time, nobody said, 'We're not going to launch COBE.' It was more about finding out how to launch it.

In the previous chapter, we met Arno Penzias, who co-discovered the cosmic microwave background radiation. You took this research further and won the Nobel Prize for investigating the infancy of the universe and the origin of galaxies and stars. Can you give us an overview of the projects you're currently working on at NASA?

I'm now working on the James Webb Space Telescope, the successor of the Hubble Space Telescope. It's much larger and more powerful than the Hubble, and it's opening up new territory. It's extremely powerful and we're able to observe exoplanets [planets outside the Solar System]. It turns out that the universe has wonderful things to show us. But it's still a relatively small telescope. Astronomers back in 1995 knew that we needed to start building bigger telescopes. So this is what we're working on now: it's been in progress all this time, and we planned to launch it.

I spend a fair amount of time talking with the public and explaining why science is interesting and exciting, especially with college students. I love talking with them.

Money-wise, what is the balance between money spent and money gained? I mean, how positive is the economic impact of a space mission?
It's a little hard to calculate: what is the value of knowledge?

In the process of developing our observatories, we invent things along the way, and we hope they'll be useful for someone else – and often they are. We also benefit from inventions by other people: we couldn't have built our space telescopes without aerospace contractors whose main business is working for other government agencies, such as the defence agency. We hire the contractors, and they help us by building telescopes.

There is a line in Brecht's Galileo saying that 'Already much has been discovered, but there is more still to be found out. And so there are always new things for new generations to do.' How do you imagine NASA in 2050?
By that time, we'll have built several new telescopes after the ones we have now. We could easily have sent people to land on Mars and bring samples for detailed analyses on the search for a sign of life there. I don't know whether we'll have found any life by then because nothing says that it's easy. We'll need to have landed in the right place on the surface to find these signs. It won't happen by chance. By then, we should be able to send researchers to other planets and perhaps have permanent places out there to monitor and understand the processes. We may be

working hard on solar physics, on what we call heliophysics, which is how the Sun influences the Earth in particular. We'll certainly be hoping to understand more about the Earth and to investigate how it's been changing and is changing over time – this is one of the most important things that people have to deal with, and what we can do about it. It's something we can work on. We'll have a very robust and important research programme in front of us for many centuries to come.

Let's talk about science diplomacy and science collaboration. Is it easier to collaborate in space than on Earth?
Collaboration is always interesting, and sometimes it's difficult. For example, in the case of the James Webb Space Telescope, we have collaborated with both Europe and Canada. From my perspective, this is a good idea. Both were contributing things that would have been hard for us to do in the United States. We could have got these things done eventually, but it's a demonstration of the importance of the work when different countries agree about that importance. When a mission runs into problems, it's easier to understand why we should keep going and make sure it happens correctly. Collaborations as opportunities will further improve in the future as long as we're interested in these possibilities. I expect much more will be done through collaborations.

Again in Brecht's Galileo: 'One cannot fly through the air on a broomstick. It must at least have a machine on it, and as yet there is no such machine. Perhaps there never will be, for man is too heavy. But, of course, one cannot tell.' How many years will it be until selfies from space from our friends appear on our social media? How far away are private journeys to space?
I don't know. There's a space agency company promising to send private astronauts around the moon pretty soon. In general, it's not too far off for space travellers. However, they need to be rich, at the moment. It's going to be a long time before it'll be inexpensive.

And would you like to be one of those space travellers?

I don't think so. In terms of the physical challenge, it's not easy to be launched into space – there's no way to avoid the 'rush' and the strenuous take-off from the ground, with the giant rockets and engines; they do something to you. A pretty good athlete could stand this, but I'm not that.

Do you have social media platforms?

I do, but I don't use them. I only scan them occasionally to see what other people are saying. I don't post things there.

I'm asking because, in the next chapter, we'll meet Brian Schmidt, who is active on Twitter. Looking back, could you ever have imagined the many things of outstanding quality you've done so far? The big fish in the little pond we were mentioning at the beginning has been rather successful.

I would never have guessed this. I couldn't have imagined I would work for NASA. The difference is that when you're at NASA, you're working with a huge team. Good ideas can be transformed into reality when there is an organization behind them. If you were a scientist just living in the countryside and working at the gas station, you might have ideas but nothing would happen. If you're at NASA, you have the chance to work with engineers and managers who are among the best in the world and can make very complex things a reality. As a young person, I wouldn't have understood that.

How important has NASA been in your life and how important have you been for NASA?

Certainly, NASA became my professional career: I have been here in Maryland for forty years. My ideas have been good, and NASA people have liked them. It's pretty clear that the ideas are more important than individual people, great as we are. It's been a great pleasure to work here and to have colleagues who have implemented these ideas, but I don't claim that the person is more important than the idea. I've always been impressed with the power of the idea.

And where do your best ideas come from?
I often think from conversations with people. When I'm sitting with my friends and talking about something, if it's an interesting idea, we can work on it or we can build it. A friend might bring you a challenge that's important enough to work on, and then you might say: 'Oh, I have an idea!' Having questions and challenges to work on is crucial, and we can try to solve them.

The magic formula then is: great ideas plus a great team.
Yes!

I read in your Nobel biography[20] that one of your interests is to write a book about Pompeii and old civilizations. Are you still planning to do this?
No, I've given up with that idea. For a while, I thought it would be fun to have a series of travel books where a tourist travelling to any big city could find information on how the technological achievements of a certain area had been accomplished. For example, if you went to Rome, you would buy a book explaining how the engineers built the Roman architecture, instead of a classical tourist book. Something like: this is how they built it, or this is how the electricity and transportation were figured out. These aspects are largely ignored, perhaps because many people don't find them interesting, but I'd be interested in them. And, at the moment, there aren't many sources where this information can be found. The same goes for cathedrals and how they were built. Think about the pyramids: we still don't know how they were built. These aspects are fascinating, but perhaps I'm not the person to write those books.

From space travel to travel in space and time, back to the history of ideas behind what we see.
One of the things that got me interested in recent years is the challenge that Darwin faced, which is where does life originate and how did it happen. NASA is now working on the question

of where life is elsewhere. And I'm reading now what other people have said.

Charles Darwin and Galileo Galilei are indeed the *fils rouge* linking the different stages of your life. What message would you send into space for other forms of life to read?
Goodness. A message to other civilizations?

Yes!
I think I have a combination of optimism and concern. Every culture faces dangers from the discoveries they make. We're meant to learn from the challenges, but whatever we invent also gives us ways to fight with each other. It's not always peaceful. The changes that we unleash with our research and the technology have been extremely challenging, and will continue to be so.

There's a science fiction story that became a movie called *Forbidden Planet*. I think it's supposed to be based on Shakespeare. The concept is that people land on a remote planet that turns out to be abandoned. The entire planet has been hollowed out and filled up with equipment. Civilization and the equipment have all disappeared. I recommend the story – it's an example of how civilization can be dangerous because we have hidden forces within us that can't easily be tamed. This is so true and it's something we face today with our global politics. Because of the way I look at the story of our origins and of how human beings have evolved as hyper-social predators, it's likely that other civilizations might evolve in the same way and will face the same challenges.

Whenever we do, we're always competing with one another. That's the concern I have, and I don't know how we're all going to overcome it. But if somebody finds this message in space, they'll know that we've solved it, at least in part.

17

À la Recherche of Space and Time

Brian P. Schmidt

The real voyage of discovery consists not in seeking new lands
but seeing with new eyes.

Marcel Proust

Professor Brian Schmidt, on the Nobel Prize website, until recently, it was written: 'Brian P. Schmidt has not submitted an autobiography.' Therefore, one of the few official biographies available was your Twitter one. Your popular account, @cosmicpinot, says: 'An overly busy Cosmologist who is Vice-Chancellor of the ANU [Australian National University], Wine maker, Dad & Husband. 2011 Nobel Laureate in Physics.' We need to know more about you. As *contrapasso*, let's start with some questions from a modified version of the Proust Questionnaire.

Your favourite virtue?

Honesty.

Your favourite occupation?

Scientist – of course!

Your idea of happiness?

Doing things that interest me.

If not yourself, who would you be?

Paul Nurse.

Where would you like to live?

Helena, Montana – although I'm very happy here in Canberra.

Your favourite writer?

Thomas Hardy.

Your favourite heroes and heroines in fiction and real life?

Hermione Granger, Indiana Jones, Marie Curie, Nelson Mandela.

Your favourite painters and composers?

Renoir, Dali, J.S. Bach, Brahms, Saint-Saëns.

Your favourite wine?

Tough call! Dom Armand Rousseau Grand Cru 2005 Chambertin.

Your favourite motto?

Do unto others as you would have done unto you.

What is your 'Proust's Madeleine', a.k.a. the object that triggers a pleasant memory from your childhood?
The closest thing I can think of is the smell of my grandparents' basement, which transports me back to my childhood instantly...

How was Brian as an undergraduate student?
I was a little lost, but mischievous. I did lots of mildly crazy or absurd things, and took lots and lots of classes because I was bored.

What were the top three crazy or absurd things you did as an undergraduate student?
Something I won't say because I fear it might be held against me, shooting rockets off the roof of Steward Observatory Building while faculty looked on, and using a large catapult to shoot oranges across the university campus.

In 1993 you obtained your PhD from Harvard University, in 1994 you settled down in Australia with your wife and in 1995 you were elected leader of the High-Z Supernova Search Team. How many people and nations were involved in that team?
When we made our discovery in 1998, there were twenty of us involved – from Australia, Chile, the USA and Germany.

The Cerro Tololo Inter-American Observatory played a paramount role in your team. How was it, working remotely in Australia with the Observatory in Chile?
In 1995, communication happened at one character per second. It was terrible. It was much better to just travel there on a plane – and that took forty-four hours door to door!

The Internet was never really good enough to work remotely and it remains challenging today. I and the others worked well together by email with the Chilean-based astronomers in terms of analysis of data, but the actual discovery programmes were essentially impossible to do remotely.

At that time, the dominating models were postulating a slowing down of the expansion of the universe, whereas you discovered the opposite. What was your hypothesis at the beginning of the project and your first reaction while analysing the data?
Our hypothesis was that we would fit a parameter called q0 – the deceleration parameter – to the data. This parameter scales directly with the density of the universe. Obviously, we thought that this parameter would show deceleration, associated with the attractive force between matter. When I first saw the dataset we eventually published in 1998, I thought we'd made some sort of terrible mistake – acceleration didn't seem like a plausible possibility. It took a couple of months for the reality of not having made a mistake to sink in.

Which parameters did you use to measure the acceleration of the expanding universe?
In the end, we needed to do a full Bayesian analysis that included the Hubble constant (although in a way in which its units were scaled out), the density of the universe in the normal gravitating matter, and the density of the universe in the form of the cosmological constant. Soon after, we also measured the equation of state of the dark energy/cosmological constant component.

In 1998, the first paper with your astonishing results was published (with Adam Riess as the first author). At the same time, the Supernova Cosmology Project led by Saul Perlmutter arrived independently at the same results. The three of you shared the Nobel Prize in 2011. But how was the competition between the two teams during those years?

The competition was pretty intense. We were competing for telescope time and came from very different cultures of research. This competition sometimes got a little less civil than it should have been, but mostly it was well behaved, with many of the various team members often being quite good friends. In the end, the competition was good for science.

You're a big Twitter fan: could you please explain your Nobel discovery in a tweet (with no more than three hashtags)?
We looked at distant exploding stars called #supernovae that exploded billions of years ago to measure how fast the #Universe was expanding back in time. We found the universe was expanding slower in the past and had sped up. #Gravity is pushing, rather than pulling, the cosmos.

What are the direct consequences of your discovery?
Our discovery indicates that seventy per cent of the universe right now comes in the form of energy that is evenly spread throughout the universe. This energy, if it persists, will make the universe expand indefinitely at an ever-increasing rate!

What were you doing when you received the call from Stockholm? What was your first reaction? Were you some-how expecting 'that' call? How did you feel?
I was in the kitchen with Jenny, my wife, helping cook dinner. I wasn't expecting the call. My first reaction was that one of my students was playing a practical joke on me. Then, as it sank in, I was overcome with a huge emotion – not unlike when my first son was born – that was so strong it made me just a little nauseous.

Is it true that you called Nobel Laureate Paul Nurse after winning the Prize? What advice did he give you?
Yes, and Peter Doherty and John Mather. I asked all three about how one might use the Prize to do good in the world, among other things, and how everything works in Stockholm.

Do you have particular anecdotes related to the Nobel ceremony in Stockholm that you'd like to share with us?

On the way to Stockholm, we got to stop and visit President Obama in the Oval Office, and on the way out, we ran into Bono, who wanted to know all about the accelerating universe. The driver who picked me up and drove me around for the week was named Stig – the same as the guy in *Top Gear*. Paul McCartney stayed in the room above me at the Grand Hotel – we heard him rattling around but didn't get to meet him. At a fancy lunch in Stockholm, we accidentally set a T-shirt on fire in a window by putting it on top of a hot light. The Crown Princess is very fun to talk to. She was six months pregnant, and her appearance at the ceremony was one of her first after her pregnancy was announced, so we got a lot of attention. Adam Riess was in the tabloids the next day with a picture of him looking at her stomach while I was talking to her.

What happened at the airport security when, on your way to visiting your grandmother in Fargo, North Dakota, your bag with the Nobel Medal was inspected?

When I won, my grandma, who lives in Fargo, North Dakota, wanted to see it. I was going to visit so I decided I'd bring my Nobel Prize. You'd think that carrying around a Nobel Prize would be uneventful, and it was until I tried to leave Fargo with it and went through the X-ray machine. I could see they were puzzled. It was in my laptop bag. It's made of gold, so it absorbs all the X-rays – it's completely black. And they'd never seen anything completely black.

They were like, 'Sir, there's something in your bag.'

I said, 'Yes, I think it's this box.'

They said, 'What's in the box?'

I said, 'A large gold medal' – as one does.

So they opened it up, and said, 'What's it made out of?'

I said, 'Gold.'

And they were like, 'Uhhhh, who gave this to you?'

'The King of Sweden.'

'Why did he give this to you?'

'Because I helped discover the expansion rate of the universe is accelerating.'

At which point, they were beginning to lose their sense of humour. I explained to them it was a Nobel Prize. Their final question was, 'Why are you in Fargo?'

What was your reaction to Bob Dylan being awarded the Nobel Prize in Literature?
I thought it was fine – inspired actually.

After having (literally) made us see the universe with new eyes, you continued your passionate campaign to promote science. You like lecturing about the universe to primary school pupils, and you're the Vice-Chancellor of the Australian National University. What are the most notable weaknesses of science teaching and of the scientific research system, and how do you think they can be overcome?
In the teaching system, I think the world lacks enough passionate well-educated teachers in science. A great teacher can make up for almost any other obstacle.

In scientific research, we have become a little too ruthless in how we approach research. We have a career structure that puts great pressure on young people and doesn't provide an environment for people to take risks in their research.

What have you learned during the last years as Vice-Chancellor of the Australian National University?
I've come to appreciate the special places that universities have in our society – something we often take for granted. The notions of academic autonomy and academic freedom are essential for us to function as the institutions we are. There are many forces on all universities to become simply factories of education and tools of the industry. While we need to

educate students and translate our research, we also need to be a place of human creativity and knowledge creation, a place where people can take a long time to ponder hard problems. Reconciling the short-term need for mass production of education and industrial research with the longer-term mission of the university is something that is ongoing here in Australia and, I think, around the world.

What is your advice for future generations of scientists?
Do what you enjoy, what you have a passion for, but put the work in to learn what you need to do to be successful.

If you were eighteen, which studies would you undertake?
For me, I might well do astronomy again, but I could easily do climate research, energy research or most probably something in big data analysis.

My advice is to make sure you get lots of maths in your education, and learn a broad range of things, including studies of everything from literature, economics and humanities to sciences you're not directly working on.

What remains to be discovered?
Ninety-five per cent of the universe. What are dark energy and dark matter? How common is life on other planets? How does gravity work with the quantum world? How did the first stars form and what were they like? Why did the universe form atoms at all and not simply a sea of photons? Why do neutrinos have mass? I could go on pretty much forever . . .

Which questions will scientists have to answer in the next fifty years?
I really don't know. I expect the new generation of telescopes will help with several of the previous questions, as will the Large Hadron Collider, possibly. But most will probably come as a surprise.

What are the next experimental challenges?
They're a mix of experimental and theoretical challenges – they play off each other. Making the new generation of

telescopes work as designed will be a huge challenge, both technically and financially. The key is to make progress experimentally for an affordable amount of money.

Science and society: you've often been vocal in championing the importance of understanding and taking actions against climate change-related issues. How would you try to convince people who still believe global warming is not an issue?

Give them a vacation for a month in Kiribati, where they can live with the people who will be the first to lose their homes to sea-level rises. They can go there via the burned Australian countryside and bleached coral reefs.

What does it mean to be a leader?

Everyone is a leader and everyone is a follower. Lead others by helping them discover what the right thing to do is.

18

Leadership and Society

Roger B. Myerson

You philosophers are lucky men.
You write on paper and paper is patient.
Unfortunate Empress that I am,
I write on the susceptible skins of living beings.

Catherine II of Russia

Professor Roger Myerson, the last sentence of your Nobel biography says: 'There is much that we still need to learn about how our social institutions operate, and how they can be better designed.'[21] This was 2007. How can today's and tomorrow's societies be better designed, both locally and globally?

In a variety of ways and for different reasons, I came to believe that we underestimate the importance of the federal distribution in government across levels. To me, countries that have failed to develop and that have fundamental political and social problems are countries that have not solved the problem of creating a constitutional *sharing* of power between national leaders and local or regional leaders. In other words, there are countries in the world that are too centralized.

Maybe the simplest way to explain this idea is from what we call industrial organization theory in economics. It is the theory of 'imperfectly competitive markets', namely markets where we buy things and where a small number of suppliers are competing. It's not a monopoly, as the consumers have alternatives. But the ideal, perfect competition doesn't exist either: there is a small number of large suppliers competing to sell us something. Maybe, what's important to make a market competitive is not so much the number of firms that are in the market. Rather, it is the ease with which, if the firms in the market reached a collusive agreement and acted as a monopoly, a new firm could come in, under-price them, get a market share and get a profit before they had lowered their prices. We call it 'low barriers to entry': the ease at which a new firm could enter the market is maybe the most important determinant.

Now let's take this idea to politics. In America and Britain, we have an electoral system that encourages two parties. This sounds like it's very close to a monopoly; it sounds less competitive than a proportional representation system with multiple parties. Are

---

[21] www.nobelprize.org

two parties enough to achieve the benefits of competition, and to achieve most of what you get from the competition? Again, it's about the 'barriers to entry': freedom of speech is about lowering barriers to entry, making it easier to organize a new political movement if our current political leaders are corrupt.

Subnational governments were also, in a critical way, lowering barriers to entry in international politics, certainly in the history of the United States. Allowing locally elected governors of provinces or mayors of cities to have a serious responsibility for public services gives them an opportunity to demonstrate their qualifications to compete for higher office.

There are many countries where democracy has spread in the past generation and it's been disappointing. Voters were excited to be able to choose their leaders and to reject leaders who performed badly. But, after a few election cycles, they discovered that they couldn't find any good leaders. They had democratically elected leaders who were as corrupt as any others and who didn't provide a good public service for less money.

What you need is not just the opportunity to choose the candidates – the candidates should also be able to develop their reputation for good public service. There have been times when the major parties at the national level were seen by the voters as all equally corrupt, certainly in American history, and so the voters have been disenchanted with all the national parties. In most years, when this has happened, a governor who was known for having done an excellent job in his state has become a strong outside-of-the-capital candidate for President. The idea is that devolving power to subnational governments, giving the main responsibilities to mayors and governors who were not appointed by the centre but elected, makes national politics more competitive. This is why national leaders in centralized countries have no incentive to devolve power to provinces or local governments, because they know that local leaders can become strong future candidates for the national leadership.

In light of this, how will or should electoral rules change in the future?

Allowing people to vote for more than one candidate in a winner-takes-all election makes the election more competitive in a variety of ways. This is called 'approval voting', and it's a very simple reform. Particularly for some aspects, such as the presidential primary, it's clearly a better way to run elections.

I'm a game theorist, and I believe the rules of the game matter. I've spoken about the importance of the distribution of power across the multiple levels of government, and that's more important, namely the federal distribution of power under any electoral system. There is also the question of presidential versus parliamentary systems. The US Federal Government suffers from having a bicameral presidential democracy. I think the British parliamentary system is much better. In Britain, more power needs to be devolved, preferably to the county level rather than at large, regional levels, because the large regions could secede to be 'nations' on their own. But I know that people who think seriously about presidential versus parliamentary systems tend to favour whichever system they're less personally familiar with. People who live under parliamentary democracies can often see the virtues of a presidential democracy better than I can.

In many countries worldwide, confidence and trust in politics and politicians are hitting an all-time low. What should be done to engage more people to participate again in political life? Is direct democracy the future?

My primary intellectual research agenda, broadly speaking, for the last twenty years has been increasingly about understanding the ecology of leadership. The first thing I think about direct democracy is that it still involves leadership. Somebody has to formulate the questions: you can't listen to more than a few hundred people all speaking at length. Maybe we should have someone totally random standing up and putting forward a motion for the budget of our village. The right to have a voice on a question such as a budget or a major change in the law is an enormous power. Inevitably, in a town meeting, most people would not be taken seriously when making such a proposal. Who are the leaders then? Who's controlling the agenda? These questions are absolutely vital. By recognizing an interaction between the different levels of government, one level of government can create leaders going to the next level.

From that perspective, town meetings can be a vital part of a nation's political system. I once had the privilege of witnessing this in a visit to Switzerland. They have an active tradition of citizens of the town getting together and talking about political issues, or at least having lead members of the town – civic leadership broadly speaking. Where such meetings exist, perhaps part of their virtue is not the decisions they make, but that the town meeting is the first level where individuals can prove themselves and then run for higher office. I don't think we should think of popular democracy as empowering the people. The question is: how do people become leaders? How can we recognize leaders at every level and how can we be sure that they face some competition from people who are proving themselves at a lower level so that they lose their status if they don't perform well? I don't look at direct democracy as a panacea. I look much more on citizens having the ability to vote and candidates having the right to run, and thinking clearly about where the next proven leaders will come from.

In 2008 you wrote: 'Sharing our planet's limited resources and building global prosperity will be impossible unless we can maintain peace throughout the world.'[22] How can we achieve this?
We've done a pretty good job so far. Somehow since World War II, or perhaps partly under the umbrella of the terrible

[22] R. B. Myerson (2008). The Power of Restraint in Strategies of Conflict and Peace. Presented as part of a panel on Challenges Facing Humanity Tomorrow in a conference organized by President Shimon Peres of Israel. https://home.uchicago.edu/~rmyerson/shalom08.pdf

nuclear arms race, wars for conquest have become almost completely globally unacceptable. Global norms have developed. We live in a time when the greatest concerns seem to be about terroristic attacks inspired by non-state groups operating from poor countries and ungovernable states. When that's your worst concern for national security, it's almost the definition of a 'golden age'. More serious concerns would be military rivalries and ultimately active military conflicts between the richest, most powerful and most productive nations on Earth. World War II was the last time we had open warfare between the most productive countries on Earth: the destructiveness was huge and people suffered enormously. The cost for humans then was, by any measure, astronomically greater than anything we're suffering today from any conflict in the world.

I'm an American citizen, so maybe people elsewhere in the world expect me to be less concerned about a world where the US is the dominant superpower. I do think that a two-superpower world has proven very dangerous. A balance of power among five major military powers could be better, although I have no theory to say any number greater than one has any stability. What we saw in a two-superpower world was both countries spending enormous sums of money, stockpiling dangerous weapons that ultimately became so powerful that they could have put at risk all multicellular life on Earth. That was a crazy thing to do. We've constantly heard in Moscow and Washington how much money the other side was spending, and what kind of dangerous weapons system they had in the other superpower, as an argument that we should spend more on a slightly more dangerous weapon system to counter them. I can't recommend that logic.

A one-superpower world existed from 1991, with the US, for whatever reason, spending more on military arms than a large number of other countries (and perhaps all the other countries in the world combined). Such a world could maintain peace if those leaders and, ultimately, the voting citizens of the US understand that this power can only be exercised with the tolerance and respect of the rest of the world. This means that the US has to use its dominant military powers according to international laws that the rest of the world can judge. And that means that the US has to submit to international judgement. I would say that for the world's sake, it might be a good thing for the US to be great in a way that's not about spending a lot of money on bigger and better weapons. That won't work.

America should exert this restraint according to international laws, which the national leaders could try to renegotiate slowly if, for example, the principles are not articulated correctly. It has to be a negotiated process with global public opinion, it has to be slow, and the US needs to be very, very predictable. If people think you might attack and destroy them unexpectedly, they'll begin spending much more of their GDP on weapons to defend themselves against America, and we'll be back to the same problem. I wish that Barack Obama, after winning his Nobel Peace Prize, had given a speech to explain to the American voters how military power needs to be non-threatening to the world. We only make it non-threatening to the world if there are restraints on the use of our own power, which should be restricted by laws and international norms that the whole world, and not just American voters, can judge.

I know you've studied the basis of the Weimar Republic. What are the key lessons you learned from that?
I am a social scientist and an idealist, and I wanted to know if what we've learned from some of the great crises of the twentieth century can make the world a safer place. In 1919, John Maynard Keynes, for example, was involved with the Treaty of Versailles at the end of World War I. The great sociologist Max Weber was corresponding with people who founded the Weimar Republic, in Germany, to establish the post-war Germany republican Constitution, after the fall of the Kaiser. There were clearly flaws in at least one of these documents,

flaws that led to the rise of Nazism and the coming of World War II. For the social scientists and politicians involved in this institutional, structural post-war negotiation, this outcome was the last thing they would have wanted.

I had a sense that there was something wrong with the Weimar Constitution. I wanted to show that the semi-presidential system in the Weimar Constitution was flawed when the Germans were adopting a new constitution without the Kaiser for the first time in 1919. They knew that there were already some parliamentary democracies and constitutional democracies in the world, so they tried to produce a structure that combined the best of both: a semi-presidential system. But you would need a theory to be able to combine the best of both, because otherwise how would you know that you were not combining the worst of both? Indeed, it's possible that they succeeded in combining the worst of both. But in the end, I felt it wasn't the Weimar Constitution's flaws that led to the rise of Nazism. Rather, it was the Reparations from the Versailles Treaty that drove Germans to empower an aggressive militaristic political movement that was determined to launch war across Europe and the world – the worst possible outcome. The flaws in the Weimar Constitution, whatever they were, were not decisive in this.

Adolf Hitler was clearly a dangerous and sick man. If you study the life of Otto von Bismarck, he also seems to have been secretly obsessed with power, but he did a pretty good job when he ran Germany. So the German people might not have been that fearful of having a dangerously power-obsessed man running the country – although, of course, Adolf Hitler was different from Otto von Bismarck. That's the historical aspect. Hitler was a bloodthirsty militant, so was attracted to the struggle of the violence. We normally don't want to have militant or bloodthirsty people running our countries, because they'd send us or our brothers or sons or husbands to die in battle. But Hitler was just one individual, however extreme. The important, fundamental question is: what drove Germans to support someone like Hitler for the leadership of their country?

We should all want to know the answer to this question, in particular because we don't want to create such conditions in the country next door to us, especially if it's more powerful than us. The answer, I think, is a deep threat to the existence and prosperity of our own country. The Reparations implicitly involved a threat to invade Germany and seize its wealth if the Germans didn't pay what they were supposed to pay in the agreement stipulated after World War I. But the threat was very abstract, and became even more abstract when the Allied troops occupying the Rhineland in Germany left the country in exchange for the government of Germany promising to pay the reparations in the future. That really was the day when Nazism became a national movement. The threat to attack Germany if they didn't pay an amount in the order of three or four per cent of their GDP annually for the next two generations became part of the political discussion. Yet it was not an immediate threat, because suddenly the Allied soldiers who could carry it out weren't there. At that point, it became safe for Germans to try to scare their enemies and the people out of that threat. They showed that they, the Germans, had chosen a bloodthirsty leader who had promised to create an arms race and that there was the probability of war being launched across their lands. Either you occupy a country and control their politics deeply, down to the lowest levels, or you respect its independence.

You're a key player in the field of game theory. Many people have watched the movie *A Beautiful Mind*, and this is, perhaps unfortunately, all that many know about game theory. Why do we generally know so little about game theory?
In the movie, there's a scene where the fictional John Nash gets his great idea, but the idea the character comes up with is awful to me. The Nash character tells the boys to go after the four girls, and that's not a Nash equilibrium, so it doesn't make any

sense. Imputing ideas that are actually illogical to a character might be an easy way to make us see him as a genius, as we can't understand how he could reach such conclusions. But what John Nash actually did was to find a coherent mathematical framework with which to represent the basic logic of conflict and cooperation.

What is true is that John Nash did make an enormous contribution to the economic and social sciences in a very short period of time when he was young. Students don't usually write papers that are a breakthrough in their field. Everyone who writes such a breakthrough paper usually does it five or eight years after they've finished being students and when they've been lecturing for some years. They find logical flaws; they learn more about how people think and how they need to be judged. John Nash is one of the very few people who had a brilliant idea at just the right time. What he truly did, and which is represented in the movie, is that he had these great ideas as a student. He then became mentally ill in a way that took him out of his field.

I was coming into the field of game theory just a few years after he left it. For the first twenty years of my life, I knew nothing about game theory. For my second twenty years, I worked on Nash's ideas while Nash was someone who was alive, but whom I could not hope to meet any more than I could have hoped to meet Julius Caesar or Christopher Columbus. But then, over the next twenty years of my life, he came back, and I got to be friends with him, and that was astonishing. The movie gives you the sense of a man who contributed but wasn't celebrated for his contribution because he'd gone. He was often in his own world, called by voices in his head. We did get to honour him, and we needed to honour him.

Now he's gone again, and in a way I could never have imagined – dying in a car accident on his way back from yet another great honour.

Triumph and tragedy were entwined in his life to the end. His life should have had more happiness. He did enjoy being recognized, but he suffered enormously. To do great work, you have to concentrate. To concentrate, you need some introspection that people could call craziness. I'm sorry that Nash's life was such that he symbolized and made manifest the suffering of the creative mind. His life was an incredible story, but it would have been a better life for him and for those he loved if he'd had a life that was not such a good story. My own life, I hope, is not going to be such a good story. I prefer my life to be just a normal, boring story.

Well, not so boring, as you changed your field of study.
I was part of a change, and I contributed to the change. The most important thing we did is what the Swedish committee called 'the mechanism design' and 'allocation mechanism'. What we were doing was thinking about the principles for recognizing and efficiently designing economic systems for a market or an organization. How can we understand social efficiency in cases where people have different information and difficulty trusting each other? The answer requires us to bring incentive constraints into the economic analysis.

We understand the world imperfectly, and we try to understand it less imperfectly. Before the 1970s, when economists were learning how to formalize the principles of economic analysis, they came to realize that we want to satisfy the needs of humans, but we have limited resources. There are resource constraints, from the quantity of oil to the number of trained physicians and the capacity of our atmosphere. Resource constraints were the centrepiece of economic theories. These constraints were mathematically associated with the market prices: that's how economists thought.

Since the 1980s, however, it's been commonplace for economists to consider incentive constraints along with resource constraints. In addition to scarce resources, we have people whose work can't necessarily be monitored by others, who have information about the potential value of some investment project, for example. Other people might not understand how valuable this might be: that's private information. We have needs and wants that other people can't necessarily monitor, and, with different information, you won't necessarily have people being honest about it. They might be giving a self-serving representation of what they know, what they want or what they need. If you ask people to contribute according to their abilities and if you give to people according to their needs, then you're going to find people saying they have a lot of needs and very few abilities. We have, therefore, to give people an incentive to reveal their real abilities and to be modest about their needs and what they ask of society.

How should we satisfy this sort of constraint? That's part of an efficiently designed social system. It has to satisfy resource constraints and incentive constraints, but it doesn't necessarily have to be a free market. I'm speaking very abstractly about constraints and the willingness of people to share information with others when they have different information. I've thought about its logic and considered some applications like auctions, but I've also thought about other abstract aspects. The average person doesn't want to know about the abstract level. However, the level of mathematical abstraction was, to me, very helpful, because there I could find the fundamental principles that we can use to connect many different applications. That's what I've been doing – that's what a theorist like me does.

For example, banks and other financial intermediaries exist because they have better information about where to invest money than depositors. The act of depositing your life savings in a bank or another financial intermediary is fundamentally a transaction between people with different information and difficulty in trusting each other. So the theory of banking is a theory that couldn't exist without our incentive-constraint revolution.

The basic principles of this revolution were developed in the 1970s when I was a graduate student: I was there at the right time for a fundamental revolution. By the early 1980s, economists who studied finance had begun developing some theories of financial intermediation using game-theory methods. Today, we need to rethink financial regulation at a fundamental level. But the principles of analysis didn't exist before the 1970s, and it wasn't until the last financial crisis that we started to rethink the foundations of macroeconomics. Macroeconomists today are far from Milton Friedman and John Maynard Keynes, but they're building on a tradition that goes back to that. John Maynard Keynes understood banks in an applied way, but he says nothing about banks in his theory. I hope we'll rebuild macroeconomics theory so that financial institutions and financial intermediaries can be central in theory in a way that they haven't been so far. There were no banks in macroeconomics theories before 1970, but there are banks in macroeconomics theories today. This doesn't mean that we know how to solve or avoid a financial crisis, but it gives me hope that the recent financial crisis will stimulate research that will lead to better policy-making in the future.

The *Encyclopaedia Britannica* says: 'At its most basic, mechanism design theory tries to simulate market conditions in such a way as to maximize gains for all parties. As buyers and sellers within a market rarely know one another's motives or ambitions, resources may be lost or misallocated because of information asymmetry. Myerson addressed this problem by proposing the revelation principle, wherein buyers are offered an incentive for truthfully reporting what they would pay for goods or services.'[23] Which social choice procedures are most likely to elicit truth-telling?

---

[23] Encyclopaedia Britannica (2007). Roger B. Myerson.
www.britannica.com/biography/Roger-Myerson

When I make a claim, you want to force me to do something to prove that the claim is true, to demonstrate how serious I am. I will call that a 'costly signal'. The mathematics of an optimal costly signal is very clear: it would be as cheap as possible for me if I was being honest, but as expensive as possible for me if I was lying. Ideally, it wouldn't have any cost, if I'm honest. That's a general theory. Michael Spencer's theory of education stated that people would spend a lot of money on education, because good, effective, responsible and talented workers of the future would succeed in an educational programme, making them more employable, even if it didn't train them to do anything more than complete a difficult educational programme. In contrast, someone who struggled in education would be seen as an irresponsible future employee.

Michael Spencer won the Nobel Prize in 2001.
I like to believe that education as part of the training I've gone through is not just about testing people, but is also about improving skills that are actually useful to make people more productive. But maybe it also serves to separate the great future leaders of our society from the not-so-great ones.

19

Of Kings and Cabbages

Robert M. Solow

The bottle, with its impotent message, was gone out to sea, and the problem that it had provoked was reduced to a simple sum in addition – one and one make two, by the rule of arithmetic; one by the rule of romance.

O. Henry

Professor Robert Solow, you're one of the most important economists ever. Is it true that the spark to study economics came from your future wife (who then became an economic historian) because she gave you positive feedback on an economics course she'd just attended?

She wasn't my *future* wife – we'd been married for two days. I'd just returned from the war and discovered that I would immediately be discharged from the Army. I had to finish my education and choose a field of study. I'd always been interested in social problems, but I needed something more specific. As usual, she made the right suggestion.

You joined the Army when you were eighteen, and you briefly served in North Africa and Italy until August 1945. What did those years teach you?

That's too long a story for me to give a serious answer. My experience taught me the importance of groups who work together with high morale. They can accomplish much more, and they're happier environments. In a similar way, I learned a lesson: do your job!

'Rome, Open City': you were sent to Rome the day before the US Army entered the city to liberate it from Nazi fascism. What feelings did you have that day? What did you see and do?

I walked into Rome on *strada statale* 6 along with five or six of my friends. We were welcomed by the people we found in a small piazza: there was much hugging and kissing and *vino rosso*. The next day we found what was then a well-known restaurant called *Fagiano*. We sat down and ordered everything on the menu (we had lire!). I sent a photograph of the *conto* [bill], which was about half a metre long, to my future wife. But then we had to rejoin our unit.

You've spent most of your academic life at the Massachusetts Institute of Technology (MIT), where you were hired in the 1950s to teach courses in statistics and econometrics. You were given the office next to Paul Samuelson, eminent economist and future Nobel Prize winner. The two of you revolutionized economics and started a life-long friendship and collaboration. In your Nobel biography, you said that your daily conversations were about 'economics, politics, our children, cabbages and kings'.[24] I understand why these conversations were on economics, politics and children, but why cabbages and kings?

Oh, that refers to a once well-known poem for children and adults. It was called 'The Walrus and the Carpenter', by Lewis Carroll. In the poem, the walrus and the carpenter 'speak of many things' and then there is a list, ending in 'cabbages and kings'. He just needed a word to rhyme with 'things'!

I see! Another quotation from the same biography, which still deals with a king (of Sweden): 'I estimate that if I had neglected the students, I could have written 25 percent more scientific papers. The choice was easy to make, and I do not regret it.'[24] *Chapeau!* Among the students you mentored, how many went to Stockholm to receive the Sveriges Riksbank Prize in Economic Sciences in Memory of Alfred Nobel?

Well, I can name George Akerlof, Peter Diamond, Paul Krugman, Robert Merton, Robert Mundell, Robert Shiller, Joseph Stiglitz and Jean Tirole. If I've forgotten anyone, I'll shoot myself. Of course, I worked more closely with some of these than with others.

Eight Nobel Prize-winning students! This must be a world record!

Give credit to the Economics Department at MIT, an excellent example of a group with high morale that functions very well.

You won the Nobel Prize in 1987 for having demonstrated how technological changes impact long-term economic

[24] www.nobelprize.org

growth. Can you please explain and contextualize what you did in simple terms?

I, like everyone else, was interested in the question: why do some economies grow faster than others in the long run? I worked out a theory that came to a surprising conclusion: under normal conditions, the only source of sustainable growth in output per worker is the progress of technology – adding more capital per worker eventually wears itself out. Then, a little later, I was able to work out a way of – roughly – measuring an economy's rate of technological progress. Of course, other economists have gone further.

You said: 'Suppose someone sits down where you are sitting right now and announces to me that he is Napoleon Bonaparte. The last thing I want to do with him is to get involved in a technical discussion of cavalry tactics at the Battle of Austerlitz. If I do that, I'm getting tacitly drawn into the game that he is Napoleon.' How many times in your life has a self-proclaimed Napoleon Bonaparte sat close to you?

Only once or twice, but that's enough.

Your opinion has been highly sought after. Among your roles, you've advised a number of US Presidents: what did you teach them and what did you learn from them? And how many times did they follow your advice?

Any President or other influential politician would be foolish to listen to just one economist (or another expert), so I will speak of 'we' meaning the profession. I think we've taught some, not all, politicians that there are limits to what even good policies can accomplish, limits determined by the way the economic system works. It's no use pretending to be able to do more. We may not know exactly where those limits are, but we may have a rough idea of how to tell when the economy is close to those limits. It seems to me that we're better at identifying bad policies and advising against them than we are at designing perfect policies. We've learned from politicians that a practical, fairly good policy is more useful than a better, but impractical, policy. Policies about spending, taxing and regulation aren't usually carried out quite the way they look on paper.

Is it true that President John F. Kennedy used to call you on the phone to ask for further information about the reports he received?

Not especially me. Walter Heller, who was Chairman of the Council of Economic Advisers in Kennedy's time, when he sent a memo to President Kennedy, would often mention which staff member had done the research. It might be me or Arthur Okun or someone else. Kennedy actually read the memos. If he found something unclear or had a question, he would sometimes call the staff member who'd done the work and ask whatever question was in his mind. This didn't happen frequently, but it did happen from time to time.

What should be done to encourage more people to participate again in political life?

I don't think I'm much of an expert on this sort of thing. I think that money has too much influence in politics in my country, and it's often used in nasty ways. Ordinary citizens of goodwill have the feeling that they don't count, or they get used in improper ways, and so they become cynical. I'm afraid that power corrupts, and this leads to more cynicism and withdrawal.

Is direct democracy the future? What are the pros and cons in your view?

I certainly hope that direct democracy is the future. It's the only political system that allows scope for human development and creativity. It's sometimes claimed that autocratic systems are more efficient. Even if that were true, it wouldn't matter: efficiency in pursuing bad goals is not a virtue. But anyway, our experience of autocracy is that it's not so efficient.

What's your opinion on the universal basic income?

A lot depends on the details of a universal basic income: how much? Who is eligible? How is it financed? To talk in generalities, a universal basic income would have some good effects and create some problems, with the good probably outweighing the bad. But if the goal is a more equal, more democratic society, then I think a universal basic income is only a small part of the solution, and other institutional changes are probably more important. I've already referred to loosening the grip of money on politics, for example. Eliminating or minimizing the educational advantages of the children of the rich is another. There are others.

What are the others you're referring to?
Reviving worker representation and collective bargaining, repairing and rebuilding cities and urban housing, perhaps partially through public-service employment.

What will be the political and social effects of increasing inequality?
Extreme inequality of income and wealth inevitably undermines the civil equality that is the basis of democracy. We tell ourselves that 'money can't buy happiness'. Perhaps, but it can buy political influence and power and, eventually, it can buy deference. And it can perpetuate itself. Extreme inequality may also generate more narrowly economic problems, like excessive saving, but it's the political and social consequences that strike me as more dangerous for democracy.

More than sixty years ago, you theorized the importance of technology in economic growth. In your vision, how will technology further impact society and the job market in the coming years?
I believe that the future of technology is very uncertain. I guess – it is a guess – that the common fear that robots will soon take all the jobs is way too dramatic. It's unlikely to happen soon, and may not happen at all. The mere possibility, however, suggests how important it would be to know who owns the robots, who profits from them, who decides what they should do. Someone should undoubtedly be thinking

about how a peaceful democratic society could function if income from work were to become a tiny part of all income.

You said: 'One standard definition of economics describes the field as the study of the allocation of scarce resources to alternative uses. That's accurate: if Adam and Eve had never left the Garden of Eden, they would never have needed an economist.' Would it have been better or worse?

Like so many things, this is a matter of preference. If the world had remained like the Garden of Eden, humanity would have avoided poverty, slavery, war and much else. But probably there would have been no Shakespeare, no Beethoven, no Einstein. I would probably have chosen the Garden of Eden, but it might have been boring.

20

Foreword to the Future

Now I think we need to move
from beautiful declarations to action.

This is why I am today here to ask and beg all of you, and
particularly young people. Young people are terribly needed
because their capacity to face problems is far better
than that of the old people.

We need to come to action: it is not enough
to make beautiful declarations,
which are all absolutely sustainable and all necessary.

It is disappointing to see that after all these declarations,
nothing has really been done.

Countless declarations, but no step has been taken forward.

Rita Levi-Montalcini at the Lindau Nobel Laureate
Meeting, 1992[25]

[25] www.mediatheque.lindau-nobel.org/laureates/levi-montalcini

Dear Reader, this text is an excerpt from an essay by Marina Keegan entitled 'The opposite of loneliness.'[26] Marina was an American author, playwright and journalist who graduated from Yale.

> *But let us get one thing straight: the best years of our lives are not behind us. They're part of us and they are set for repetition as we grow up and move to New York and away from New York and wish we did or didn't live in New York. I plan on having parties when I'm 30. I plan on having fun when I'm old. Any notion of THE BEST years comes from clichéd 'should haves ...' 'if I'd ...' 'wish I'd ...'*
>
> *Of course, there are things we wished we did: our readings, that boy across the hall. We're our own hardest critics and it's easy to let ourselves down. Sleeping too late. Procrastinating. Cutting corners. More than once I've looked back on my High School self and thought: how did I do that? How did I work so hard? Our private insecurities follow us and will always follow us.*
>
> *But the thing is, we're all like that. Nobody wakes up when they want to. Nobody did all of their reading (except maybe the crazy people who win the prizes ...) We have these impossibly high standards and we'll probably never live up to our perfect fantasies of our future selves. But I feel like that's okay.*
>
> *We're so young. We're so young. [...] We have so much time. There's this sentiment I sometimes sense, creeping in our collective conscious as we lay alone after a party, or pack up our books when we give in and go out – that it is somehow too late. That others are somehow ahead. More accomplished, more specialized. More on the path to somehow saving the world, somehow creating or inventing or improving. That it's too late now to BEGIN a beginning and we must settle for continuance, for commencement.*

[26] M. Keegan (2012). The opposite of loneliness. *Yale Daily News.* https://yaledailynews.com/blog/2012/05/27/keegan-the-opposite-of-loneliness/

When we came to Yale, there was this sense of possibility. This immense and indefinable potential energy – and it's easy to feel like that's slipped away. We never had to choose and suddenly we've had to. Some of us have focused ourselves. Some of us know exactly what we want and are on the path to get it; already going to med school, working at the perfect NGO, doing research. To you I say both congratulations and you suck.

For most of us, however, we're somewhat lost in this sea of liberal arts. Not quite sure what road we're on and whether we should have taken it. If only I had majored in biology... if only I'd gotten involved in journalism as a freshman ... if only I'd thought to apply for this or for that ...

What we have to remember is that we can still do anything. We can change our minds. We can start over. Get a post-bac or try writing for the first time. The notion that it's too late to do anything is comical. It's hilarious. We're graduating college. We're so young. We can't, we MUST not lose this sense of possibility because in the end, it's all we have. [. . .] We're in this together. Let's make something happen to this world.

Acknowledgements

I am extremely grateful to each and every Nobel Laureate who enthusiastically accepted the invitation to be interviewed for this book. It has been a unique privilege and a great honour for me: I have enjoyed every moment and I have learned a lot. I would like to express my great appreciation and my special thanks to the Lindau Nobel Laureate Meetings and Nikolaus Turner, Managing Director, who endorsed and supported this project. Many thanks to Countess Bettina Bernadotte, Council President, for her Foreword and for keeping the Lindau dream alive for future generations of young scientists. *Dankeschön* to Gero von der Stein and Wolfgang Haaß, past and current Head of Communications in Lindau, for their support. Finally, thanks to Katrina Halliday, Jane Hoyle and Jenny van der Meijden at Cambridge University Press.

Appendix:
List of Nobel Laureates

Peter Agre	Nobel Prize in Chemistry 2003
Françoise Barré-Sinoussi	Nobel Prize in Physiology or Medicine 2008
Elizabeth H. Blackburn	Nobel Prize in Physiology or Medicine 2009
Martin Chalfie	Nobel Prize in Chemistry 2008
Aaron Ciechanover	Nobel Prize in Chemistry 2004
Johann Deisenhofer	Nobel Prize in Chemistry 1988
Richard R. Ernst	Nobel Prize in Chemistry 1991
Edmond H. Fischer	Nobel Prize in Physiology or Medicine 1992
David J. Gross	Nobel Prize in Physics 2004
Roald Hoffmann	Nobel Prize in Chemistry 1981
Tim Hunt	Nobel Prize in Physiology or Medicine 2001
Daniel Kahneman	Sveriges Riksbank Prize in Economic Sciences in Memory of Alfred Nobel 2002

Eric R. Kandel	Nobel Prize in Physiology or Medicine 2000
John C. Mather	Nobel Prize in Physics 2006
Kary B. Mullis	Nobel Prize in Chemistry 1993
Roger B. Myerson	Sveriges Riksbank Prize in Economic Sciences in Memory of Alfred Nobel 2007
Arno Allan Penzias	Nobel Prize in Physics 1978
Venkatraman Ramakrishnan	Nobel Prize in Chemistry 2009
Randy W. Schekman	Nobel Prize in Physiology or Medicine 2013
Brian P. Schmidt	Nobel Prize in Physics 2011
Hamilton O. Smith	Nobel Prize in Physiology or Medicine 1978
Robert M. Solow	Sveriges Riksbank Prize in Economic Sciences in Memory of Alfred Nobel 1987
Roger Y. Tsien	Nobel Prize in Chemistry 2008
Torsten N. Wiesel	Nobel Prize in Physiology or Medicine 1981

Credits

The author acknowledges the following for quotations within chapters:

Chapter 1: *Ithaka*, from C. P. Cavafy: Collected Poems, Revised Edition, translated by Edmund Keeley and Philip Sherrard, edited by George Savidis.

Chapter 1: Primo Levi, *The Periodic Table*, Little, Brown & Co., London, 1984.

Chapter 7: T. R. Poston, 'Augusta Savage', Metropolitan Magazine, January 1935, n.p.

Chapter 8: © Bridget Riley.

Chapter 9: © Albert Einstein.

Chapter 13: © Barbara McClintock.

Chapter 14: © Duke Kahanamoku.

Chapter 16: © Bertolt Brecht (1938), from *Life of Galileo*, translated by Mark Ravenhill, Methuen Drama, an imprint of Bloomsbury Publishing Plc.

Chapter 20: © Rita Levi-Montalcini at the Lindau Nobel Laureate Meeting, 1992. www.mediatheque.lindau-nobel.org/laureates/levi-montalcini

Chapter 20: M. Keegan (2012). The opposite of loneliness. *Yale Daily News*. https://yaledailynews.com/blog/2012/05/27/keegan-the-opposite-of-loneliness/

Index